the Master's touch

volume II

by DOROTHY SOUTH HACKWORTH

ISBN: 1-55517-041-2

Published and distributed in the United States of America
by:

Cedar Fort, Inc.
1182 North Industrial Park Road
Orem, UT 84057

Lovingly dedicated
to my husband
HUBERT EDGAR HACKWORTH
and to our children
SHIRLENE
ALLEN
REGINA
LOIS
DONNA
GERALD

Table of Contents

PREFACE

This book is the result of the efforts of many persons, including those of the publisher.

Since 1980, the author has desired to compile a "few" more experiences and selected testimonies to uplift the lives of others.

Initially, Mrs. Hackworth determined that if Steven Hawkes and Cody and Dave Atkinson would share their precious stories, she would become engrossed in producing a second volume.

As was the case with *The Master's Touch*, Volume 1, the "few" snowballed into many other choice experiences.

Sensing that it is never idle repetition to say that God lives and that Jesus Christ is the Son of God, she has attempted to capture and preserve stories that will remind concerned individuals of the welfare of those around us and the over-all goodness of a loving Heavenly Father.

This effort—though perhaps feeble—is an effort to follow the instructions of our Heavenly Father to be "anxiously engaged in a good cause, and do many things of (our) own free will, and bring to pass much righteousness;

"For the power is in (us) wherein (we) are agents unto (ourselves). And inasmuch as men do good they shall in nowise lose their reward."

It is the author's fervent hope that this communication will help the reader sense the good that others are doing and the good the reader is capable of that we may all secure our rewards.—D.S.H.

Part One

TESTIMONIES

from

NEAR AND FAR

"And again I speak unto you, who deny the revelations of God, and say they are done away, that there are no revelations, nor prophecies, nor gifts, nor healings, nor speaking in tongues. Behold I say unto you, he that denieth these things, knoweth not the Gospel of Jesus Christ; yea, he has not read the scriptures; if so, he does not understand them."

—Mormon 9:7,8.

THE TOUCH OF THE MASTER'S HAND

As a young father of one daughter and five sons and an avid sportsman, former athletic coach, and friend of youth, I find it still amazing how one event, nearly a decade ago, could teach me more about spiritual awareness in a few hours than I had contemplated in a lifetime. Since then, I have become aware of how the Lord's hand has been with me since birth. It took a tragedy in the icy waters of Shoshone Lake to bring about this awareness.

The summer of 1978 was like any other summer. School was out. As a teacher at South Fremont High School in St. Anthony, Idaho, I eagerly awaited the three summer months. During the summer I was groundskeeper for the school district, and I was excited to get on the tractor, mow the lawns, and take care of the grounds. I was also excited about visiting Shoshone Lake for the eighth summer in a row. It is located in the south central portion of Yellowstone National Park. I had fallen in love with its pastoral setting and the magic spell it had cast over my life. Having grown up in the mountains of Wyoming, I felt at home where I could see God's great creations and beauties, relax, and escape the complexities of our modern world. The summer would bring a series of events that would change my life.

Unknown to me, the Master took me by the hand and gently prepared me for seven weeks prior to this long-awaited, five-day adventure.

In eagerness I began to plan and prepare. My good friend, Darrel Gibbons, bishop of the Parker Ward, and his father, Ray Gibbons, a Utah dairy farmer, would accompany me, along with my two oldest sons, Craig 12, and David, 8. Rowing across Lewis Lake and walking the canoes up a three-and-a-half-mile river to get to Shoshone Lake would require both strength and stamina, so for the first time in several years, I began to condition myself. For some reason, I had never before felt the need to train. I ran two miles every morning before work and was in the best shape of my life; it felt wonderful. Darrel was also in excellent physical condition.

As the middle of July approached, we almost cancelled our trip to Shoshone Lake because of a stake championship softball game in which Darrel and I were to play against each other. But instead of playing, for some unknown reason, we decided to follow our former plans.

We went to Yellowstone, secured our backcountry permits, licensed the canoes, and spent the morning of July 19 rowing across Lewis Lake to shoshone Lake. The weather was beautiful for this time of the year. We saw moose, otter, and heard some elk bugling through the forest. We set up camp and spent the rest of the day gathering wood, trout fishing, and eating. The next morning we did more of the same, relaxed, and immensely enjoyed each other's company. We also slept and dozed a lot. Craig and David were having a great time.

About noon we noticed black clouds in the west and knew a storm was imminent. We beached the canoes and built up a big fire, hoping the storm would blow over. It was then we noticed five brightly-colored canoes entering Shoshone Lake and heading directly west. Their destination seemed several miles ahead. We watched, hoping the lake wouldn't become too rough since they were heading into the middle of it. By afternoon, ominous clouds formed and extremely high winds gusted. Never had I witnessed a storm come up so suddenly with such power. It was like a hurricane had hit, and immediately the lake turned into a towering, watery inferno.

We watched the five helpless canoes head into the fury of the storm. (Earlier that Thursday, July 20, eight Explorer Scouts and their two leaders from the Wilford, Ward had set out for Shoshone Lake. Each canoe was navigated by a team of two. They consisted of Kim Bischoff and Brant Kerbs; Van Hansen and Lane Potter; David Bischoff and Wade Singleton; Daren Dayton and Darris Williams; and their leaders, Layne Reynolds and John Bischoff, Kim's father.

At first we could see five canoes, then four, then three, and eventually none. We became alarmed because of the fierceness of the explosive storm and the unbelievably high waves. We hoped we had only lost sight of them. After many anxious minutes, we saw a canoe coming toward our Moose Creek campsite. It was more than a mile away, but we were grateful to know something was still afloat. Due to the ferocity of the storm and the canoe riding the waves, it soon reached us. The waves beached it on dry land. As we ran down to the beach, two young men turned around and horror entered my soul. "Kim Bischoff!" I said.

"Coach Sam, what are you doing here?" Kim exclaimed.

Then the realization hit. They were from the Wilford Ward. We hurried Kim and Brant to the warmth of the campfire and quickly got their story. Daren and Darris had swamped as had possibly another canoe. They didn't know about the others, except that they had seen a determined Van Hansen and Lane Potter paddling toward shore.

Darrel had taught these young men and the others facing a life-and-death crisis in seminary classes, and I had taught them history and U.S. government at South Fremont, thus endearing them to us.

We built up the fire and seriously pondered our next move. Each of us prayed silently for help. Within an hour we spotted another canoe coming our way. This one moved more slowly. When it was about a half mile away it, too, capsized and tossed its passengers, Layne Reynolds, John and David Bischoff, and Wade Singleton, into the icy forty-two-degree-water. This canoe had picked up Layne Reynolds and John Bischoff, who had also been thrown into the water.

As Darrel and I raced to the beach in the fury of the storm, the first and second of many spiritual experiences unfolded. We knelt at once in prayer and humbly petitioned Heavenly Father for divine guidance, strength, and protection. Within seconds, a voice came to me as clearly and audibly as if from my own lips. It said, "Go, and ye shall be protected."

Encouraged by this personal and inspired confirmation, we immediately ran back to get a canoe. Then as if planned, Darrel's father appeared and suggested we lash two canoes together for greater stability. He had seen it done many years before. Since we had no poles, we quickly tied three extra paddles together, along with three hundred feet of extra rope we had brought for no apparent reason. We tried two unsuccessful launches. After almost thirty minutes of unsuccessful attempts, we finally succeeded. It was tediously slow and nearly impossible to go against the gale forces of the wind. I compared our plight to the ship on the Sea of Galilee when our Savior rode an angry storm. Our double-rescue canoe lurched almost straight up at the first wave, throwing me backwards into the water. Totally drenched, I made a quick recovery and climbed into the canoe more determined than ever.

We finally approached the first of the boys in the water, David Bischoff. He took one look at me and yelled, "Oh, no, I'm dead!" I told him he wasn't, but he said, "I must be, because I thought I saw Coach Sam."

We also found Wade Singleton and Layne Reynolds and brought the three to camp. It was terrifying. They were all in shock. Layne was virtually helpless from advanced hypothermia. we were grateful to be able to give them a priesthood blessing and treat their critical needs. A calm engulfed us as we suddenly comprehended why we had been sent to Shoshone Lake at this particular time.

Kim Bischoff again came to me, sobbing, "My father is gone. He is gone!"

We hadn't been able to locate him after rescuing the other three. Barely conscious, John had seen the canoe leave and felt all was lost.

With a heavy heart, I walked to the beach. There a glorious vision opened before my eyes. I saw Kim's father some three-fourths of a mile in the lake. He appeared cold, but he was alive! I ran back and told Darrel that we must search for John. No one else could see him, but I could still see him and his exact location. We spent the next hour rescuing him. He was incoherent and unable to recognize anyone. With muscles paralyzed from over two and one half hours in the icy water, he could offer no assistance. He weighed over two hundred pounds, so it was not easy to get him into our canoe, but we pulled him to safety like a water-soaked log.

Propelling our double-hulled canoe toward shore, fighting our way back through the towering waves, we worried about the boys still on the lake. We knew over three hours had passed since Daren and Darris had tipped into the water; and if they were to be found before dark, it had to be soon. Lane and Van were last seen approaching the north shore. We hoped they were safe beside a crackling fire.

Arriving at camp, we found many willing and helping hands waiting to assist with John. Kim asked for a priesthood blessing for his father who was not at that time a member of the Church. Many more inspired priesthood blessings were given that day. As John slowly responded to treatment, we prepared to go hunt for Darris and Darren, Lane and Van. We really felt there was no way we could locate them or know what had happened to them.

As the winds decreased, Darrel came running back and said he had spotted another group. I couldn't see anything, but agreed to again go searching. This time Ray Gibbons and Kim Bischoff accompanied Darrel and me in our little life-boat. Darrel and I were almost physically exhausted.

As we approached an upturned canoe, we saw Daren and Darris with their arms locked together. They were completely unconscious. They had anticipated death. Their exposure covered an incredible four and a half hours. Suffering advanced hypothermia, the young men fought to live. Daren was pulled to safety first. Darris fought to hang onto the canoe as if it were life itself. Finally Darrel loosened Darris' grip and lifted him into the boat. We rushed to a campsite and built a huge fire. For the next two hours we massaged their bodies and did everything we could remember from scout first aid training. I know it was through the power of the priesthood exercised that night that two more young men miraculously escaped death.

We searched and searched for the two remaining Explorers, but it became dark. After 12:30 a.m. when we were finally back and in our sleeping bags, we still kept wondering and praying for the welfare of Lane and Van.

The next morning Darrel and his father arose early and walked along the beach. They discovered some supplies lost from the canoes. Then they saw it—Van and Lane's overturned green canoe. Darrel stared in utter disbelief, then pulled it ashore. Heartsick, they walked back to camp. I felt devastated. Darrel and I went to a forest ranger's cabin for help. It was locked. A hiker passing though the area volunteered to hike to the ranger station at Grants Village several miles across the mountains to the east to report the missing boys. Within an hour a helicopter hovered over Moose Creek Camp and landed. A ranger stepped out and confirmed that a body had been found. It was later identified as Lane Potter. Van Hansen's body was found the following day.

My heart ached for the parents of these young men. I knew they would experience the worst kind of grief. I cried and hurt deeply for them. I thought I could understand the anguish, hurt, and bitterness that would accompany this tragedy. But now I know I couldn't. Four years later, on August 23, 1982, my beloved wife, Janice, and I lost our six-year-old John who accidentally drowned. I then could appreciate what these stunned, courageous parents felt.

Darrel and I continue to share our feelings and express heartfelt gratitude to Heavenly Father in directing the perilous rescue we and the others performed, for had we failed, all woud have perished. Only a tenth part of what really transpired has been written here. This experience has built testimonies and added depth and meaning to many lives. I know that the spiritual overtones for two young boys, a father for his son, and two close friends will undoubtedly be engrained in our lives forever. It certainly has shown to me, and I feel sure to all who were involved, the touch of the Master's hand.

Sam Christiansen
January, 1987

Lane's mother, Wanda Potter, relates her feelings:
        The Scouts and their leaders from Wilford had planned this exciting and challenging outing for a long time.
        These young men were excited about life, always giving one hundred percent to everything they did. They began playing Peewee ball together at age eight. Their team had eighteen boys. An added treat was having Lane's father and Darren Dayton's father coach them. Their summers were fun and exciting as they struggled, learned, accomplished, and succeeded at the game of ball and of life. They became a great bunch of players, always caring about each other and everyone around them.
        The Class of 1980 was probably as caring a group of students as had ever graduated from South Fremont High School. The Wilford gang of boys always had a great time. There were several brothers in the group including two sets of twins.
        Initially, Lane's twin brother, Shane, and Van Hansen's brother, Jan, were going to Shoshone Lake, but not Lane and Van. However, their plans changed, and

only Lane and Van went. We realized later that this change was part of the Lord's plans for these young men's lives.

My husband, Frank, and I felt very nervous about the boys going, but they convinced us they should go. As they prepared to leave that morning, we made Lane and Van promise they would wear their life jackets. When we heard the news that the boys were missing and not wearing life jackets, we were heartsick. We felt they probably would not be found as had been the case in some instances. But when they were located, they did indeed have them on.

The same day the Scouts left for Shoshone Lake, a friend of mine, Carol Dayton, and her daughter, Jerrice; my daughter, Jalene; and I left St. Anthony for Bountiful, Utah, to take Jalene to a friend's wedding. Jalene remained there; Carol, Jerrice and I planned to attend the Mormon Miracle Pageant in Manti, so we traveled on. This was another event by which the Lord helped Frank, our family, and me prepare for what was to happen.

It was raining in Manti, but as the pageant's starting time arrived, the rain ceased, and conditions were favorable. As the pageant proceeded, about 9:00 p.m. I felt very tired, and a great heavy feeling came over me. Yet, as the scenes continued and portrayed death's part in the plan of life, it was very vivid to me. I felt a marvelous understanding of death and its purpose. Because it had been impossible to contact me, I learned about eight the following night of Lane's untimely accident. I realized then that I had felt his passing at this particular time.

Frank and I gained a great and deep love for Jesus Christ, recognizing the part he plays in each of our lives and that through him our son could receive eternal life. Many times we have felt his sustaining influence. As the hours and days afterwards seemed unbearable, our family and friends and our dear Father in Heaven carried us through.

The circumstances surrounding this outing made us realize that this experience was according to God's plan. Many incidents later revealed by both the leaders and the other young men involved confirmed our testimonies and feelings. We know it was God's will for Lane and Van to continue their missions in another sphere.

It is never easy to part with a loved one, especially one so young. Understandably, at first we were terribly distressed, but we continually feel grateful for the sixteen years we had Lane and for the glorious knowledge that we can be together as a family again through our obedience and faithfulness. Certainly this makes parting more bearable and comforting. To us, it seems many gentle lessons were taught to others as well as during and after this sobering and seemingly tragic event.

Wanda Potter

October 27, 1987

I WALK BY FAITH

I was born in 1932, at Las Vegas, Nevada. My parents, Martin Laurell Johnson and Elva Lorena Rasmussen, were happy and excited over my arrival. But what a shock it must have been for Martin and Elva to learn their baby girl, Cleta Marianne, was blind.

They taught me the principles of life. Mother has given a life of service to others but especially has tended to my every need. Father, until his death, loved me deeply. I am grateful for their help and support, also for that of my family and dear, deceased grandparents.

I look on my blindness as a blessing. It has changed the lives of others, particularly my parents, in a positive way.

I recall with delicious memory, my father swimming with me on his back, out to what he called the "pilings" at Lake Meade. I knew no fear. I loved and trusted him. I had no idea where he was swimming in that deep, deep water. I knew nothing of life preservers in those days. All I knew was that I was on Daddy's back, gliding like a fish in that big lake. When we got to the pilings, he told me to reach out and hold on. He assured me he would be close by as he swam all around me. When he returned, I climbed on his back again, and away we went. The most fun of all was when he said, "Take a deep breath; we're going under the water." I loved it! As soon as we surfaced, I would exclaim, "Do it again, Daddy, do it again." How sweet to remember the exciting beauty of it all and the joy of my simple child-like faith.

With this same simple faith, I have proceeded through life. My blindness frequently places me in the hands of or at the mercy of, others. In those instances, too, I am trusting, for I *must* walk by faith.

No one appreciates the hand of another more than I—the helpful hand of the stranger, desiring to be of assistance, even knowing my guide dog is capable, the hand of a loved one touching mine in that gentle unspoken communication only loved ones can know. I appreciate the hand of a Tabernacle Choir sister, communicating the exact moment to raise or lower my music folder during broadcast or when to stand or sit in concert.

I am grateful for strong hands holding the Melchizedek Priesthood that have been placed on my head giving me needed blessings from our beloved heavenly Father, blessings that have comforted me and miraculously healed me.

I am most appreciative for the hand of the Lord in my life—that gentle, unseen hand, guiding me, not with force, but with his all-encompassing love. How comforting it is to know no matter how far away he may seem to be, he is very close. He has often intervened in my life, in times of danger, sorrow, trouble, and stress.

Truly, throughout my life, I have walked by faith using my intelligence and common sense. Now it is with my beautiful guide dog. In the past, it was with a white cane or with the hand of my parents, other relatives and friends, and the caring stranger. I want to tell you about Tracy.

In the summer of 1972, as I stood on a street corner in North Hollywood, California, a million thoughts raced through my mind. The most paramount was,

"Take courage, Marianne, you can do it! You weren't killed before." Yet, I wondered, "What about now? What about this time?" This assignment was one of the most challenging of my life. Knowingly and purposefully, I was about to cross the street in front of a speeding automobile—"sheer suicide," I thought. Yes, this was what I had to do within the next few seconds.

I was nearing the completion of twenty-eight days of training in guide dog school. My beautiful German shepherd guide dog, Tracy, stood at my left side, ever watchful, ever waiting—anxiously listening for her name, followed by her next command from me. Tracy's harness was securely in my hand. I was in proper stance and alignment to cross this formidable street. To my right was the assistant dog trainer, who at any second now, would be placing his hand on my shoulder. This was my signal to say, "Tracy, forward!"

As I heard the speeding car approaching, I was gripped with sudden terror. "No one in their right mind would want to step out in front of a moving vehicle," I thought. The car came closer. Then the inevitable—the trainer's hand was gently, yet firmly, placed on my shoulder. There was no turning back.

With all the courage I had and with authority and conviction, I commanded, "Tracy, forward!"

Much to my relief, as the car sped by, Tracy did not move so much as a paw off the California curb. My instantaneous pats and praises for Tracy were received with a happy wagging tail. She had done her job well.

This traffic check was the final phase of our training. Before any student can graduate from Erich Renner's Guide Dog School with his dog, he must meet the challenge of the traffic check. Erich, himself, wearing blindfolds goes through this traffic check with every dog that leaves his school. There can be no question or doubt,

nor any room for error—no chance for a costly life-
threatening mistake. The dogs must be expertly trained. I
was worthy to graduate, which I did at the top of the
class. Through diligence and hard work Erich Renner
had turned out another fine team, my sixty-pound Tracy,
and me. She was really the star!

Later that night, packing for our trip back to Salt
Lake City, I smiled as I recalled Tracy's perfect
performance. I paused to cuddle her. We were just
beginning a sharing, caring experience that would last for
several years. As I thanked our beloved Heavenly Father
that night, I was grateful to have not only one of the
most beautiful guide dogs ever to graduate, but one of
the most intelligent and obedient as well. I was
particularly grateful for Erich Renner's expert training
and concern. Also, I appreciated knowing that Tracy and
I could walk with confidence having implicit faith and
trust in each other.

This experience with one of my four guide dogs is
but one of many I could share where truly I have walked
by faith.

Although I have lived with physical blindness
through the years, there is a vast difference between
physical blindness and spiritual blindness. How grateful I
am that I am not among the spiritually blind. I am
humbly proud to be a member of that great and glorious
church, The Church of Jesus Christ of Latter-day Saints,
and to know that I know it is true.

I would say to the spiritually searching: You, too,
can know for a surety as do I and millions of other
Latter-day Saints that this blessed gospel of Jesus Christ is
true. Read for yourselves. Do the things the scriptures
counsel us to do. Keep the Lord's commandments.
Follow the admonitions of the prophets from the

beginning down and to including our current prophet, Ezra Taft Benson. They are the mouthpiece of the Lord.

When I was a young girl in grade school, one of my favorite teachers, Caroline Parry, (now deceased), often shared a favorite saying with us. "There is none so blind as those who will not see!" So let's hold fast to that which is good. A testimony is so fragile, as fragile as a tiny bird. Just as we need food every day for our physical bodies, so also we require strengthening, nourishing spiritual food. But it takes faith, faith to take the first step toward returning to God's presence by accepting the gospel. Faith is to have complete trust, confidence, or reliance. How simple are those three words, yet how profound.

Next is repentance, followed by baptism and confirmation into the Church, a passport to heaven.

At first, you will walk by faith, gradually evolving into the spiritual awareness that today's faith will soon become tomorrow's knowledge. We all must walk by faith down the corridors of life, but such faith will one day bring us into the light of eternity, into the everlasting presence of our Father in Heaven, the Father of our spirits. As the ancient prophet Alma counsels in the Book of Mormon, let the seed of faith be planted in your heart, and begin to swell within your breast.

"And now behold, if ye nourish it with much care it will get root, and grow up, and bring forth fruit" (Alma 32:37).

As I continue to walk with my faithful German shepherd beside me, so also I continue to walk with my faithful shepherd, Jesus Christ, by my side. Our Savior walks by your side as well. May you have that sweet reassuring trust and confidence in your reliance on him as you walk by faith.

Marianne J. Fisher
August, 1986

C. Marianne Johnson Fisher is the author and composer of "As I Search the Holy Scriptures" (*Hymns*, 1985, no. 277.)

AS I SEARCH THE HOLY SCRIPTURES

As I search the holy scriptures,
Loving Father of mankind,
May my heart be blessed with wisdom,
And may knowledge fill my mind.

As I search the holy scriptures,
Touch my spirit, Lord, I pray.
May life's mysteries be unfolded
As I study day by day.

As I search the holy scriptures,
May thy mercy be revealed.
Soothe my troubled heart and spirit;
May my unseen wounds be healed.

As I search the holy scriptures,
Help me ponder and obey.
In thy word is life eternal;
May thy light show me the way.

THE LORD HAD A WORK FOR ME TO PERFORM

I'm positive the Lord directs our lives, motivating us to do good works or assist in the building up of his kingdom; and his purposes are fulfilled.

I didn't recognize Heavenly Father's influence in my life until I was in my first year of college at Ricks in Rexburg, Idaho. I was there mostly because of the admonition of my kind and patient mother. It was at the height of the Vietnam War era. My parents feared I would fall into the wrong crowds at college and not live up to my potential. Consequently, they wished me to be educated at a conservative school.

We first applied to Brigham Young University because of its excellent music opportunities. Music had always been a love of mine. However, my grade point average wasn't acceptable. Along with a letter of rejection from BYU, I received a flyer for application to Ricks College. My mother filled out the application, never losing hope in me, even when I did. I interpreted the flyer to mean that the school's motto was "give me your tired, your poor . . . your huddled masses of underachievers." I honestly felt Dad and Mom were trying to find a place far away to isolate me and to get me out of their hair.

However, I was overjoyed at being accepted. My parents accompanied me out to "the land of desolation" (as called by students from Utah) in August, 1970. First impressions are interesting. I thought Rexburg was a typical small town in the middle of nowhere.

After the initial shock of my parents' departure and a sampling of campus atmosphere, I was convinced I had made one of the worst mistakes of my life. Sometimes a person can't see the forest while in the thick of it. Maybe it was fear or insecurity. I don't know, but as school progressed, my fear vanished.

One afternoon during the fall semester, two men came to my hotel room. I recognized them as my college professors, Ron Messer and Darwin Wolford. Darwin was a music professor and Ron was an English teacher. They were stake missionaries sent by the landlady of my hotel. I had no idea they were missionaries. I was too flabbergasted that two college professors were taking time out of their busy schedules to visit me, a lowly freshman. They said that they understood I was not a Mormon and wondered if I would be interested in learning a little about the history and ideas which made Mormons unique. Of course, I invited them in. Over the next several months I learned from them first-hand about The Church of Jesus Christ of Latter-day Saints.

At the end of the discussions, they challenged me to baptism. I declined. But their words stayed with me, and I recognized the spirit I felt in their presence on other occasions.

The second semester I decided to take a Book of Mormon class. It began with the book of Alma. As class commenced that semester, nothing seemed out of the ordinary. We were given reading assignments. During the following class, we discussed what was read, and the instructors interjected comments.

Then, late one evening in January, 1971, while I was lying on my bed reading from the Book of Mormon, I read Alma 7:15.

"Yea, I say unto you come and fear not, and lay aside every sin, which easily doth beset you, which doth bind you down to destruction, yea, come and go forth, and show unto your God that ye are willing to repent of your sins and enter into a covenant with him to keep his commandments, and witness it unto him this day by going into the waters of baptism."

Never had I been so affected by the printed word. All at once, I began to have the strangest sensation—as if someone had turned up the temperature setting on my electric blanket. I felt a warmth in my chest that was so storng it made me clutch my nightshirt. I even checked my electric blanket to see if it was turned higher than I usually set it. But to my surprise, the blanket was not even plugged into the wall socket. It was then that the words of the missionaries came back to me as if they had just spoken them. "The Spirit will testify to you of the truthfulness of these things by causing your bosom to burn."

That's exactly what happened. I had known of the truthfulness of the gospel ever since the missionaries came to my door. But I had not come to this realization because I was comfortable in my present environment. I enjoyed my lifestyle, my vices, my freedom from religion and commitment. But this scripture reminded me that by failing to commit to be baptized, I was allowing myself to be bound to my past instead of beginning with a clean slate and serving the Lord.

I was overjoyed with my revelation and wished to share my happiness with those in the hotel. But because of the late hour, as I ran down the hallway shouting that I wanted to be baptized, I received little response, with the exception of an "all right already . . . go to bed!"

The next day I contacted Professor Messer to schedule my baptism. He informed me that because of my age, I needed my parents' approval. I immediately decided to pray and fast for the Lord to soften their hearts and grant my desire. At the end of my fast that evening, I called my parents in Chicago and asked their permission. They said they were not surprised, considering my close interaction with the LDS people, adding that if it would make me happy, they wouldn't mind in the least.

I made peanut butter and honey sandwiches with homemade bread to celebrate their answer and end my fast and shared them with Professor Messer.

I was baptized on January 28, 1971, in the Rexburg Tabernacle baptismal font. It was a memorable evening service with friends and classmates there. My good friends, Richard (Jody) Clayton Robson baptized me, and Roger Little confirmed me a member of the Church.

I graduated with a junior college degree in music education in May 1972. From there I transferred to BYU, which proved to be a totally different experience for me. The campus was large, and the people seemed distant and preoccupied. Even though I had a testimony of the gospel, I found it increasingly difficult to be a Christian when others were cold in their relationships. Not all students and teachers were that way, but the difference seemed overwhelming compared to those friendly members of the Church I had met in Idaho.

I transferred from a music education major to music theory. I even entered and placed in the "Mormon Festival of Arts" music composition contest in March, 1973. In order to always be reminded of my talents as a composer, I bought a turquoise ring with my prize money.

Unfortunately, as time went on, I allowed myself to be negatively affected by others around me who did not live the gospel as I felt it should be lived. I pulled away from activity. Other mistakes followed: my accepting a Sunday job and moving into an apartment without roommates. I even registered on campus as having a post office box out of town so nobody could find me.

After graduation from BYU in 1975, I moved back to Chicago with two cats to live with my parents.

Because of some bad experiences with people who I felt had been un-Christlike to me, I decided not to go to church and keep to myself. That costly mistake took me four years to correct. I learned that one should never judge the gospel by Church members. The gospel is perfect. The people are not. Wicked people are found everywhere; even with the Church, at times, even in callings of prominence. We should never allow others' actions to affect our eternal destiny!

During those four years of inactivity, I met Susan Lynn Rieth, married her, and worked in several occupations from stock boy to truck driver to computer operator and repairman for a typesetting firm. During that time, I received home teachers occasionally. The same home teachers never visited more than twice without being reassigned. I wasn't hostile. I just wasn't ready to make that commitment again. Nor was I ready to forgive my offenders.

Then, someone came by one day, and announced that he was my home teacher. His name was Ryan Trimble. He respected me and never talked about religion until I was ready. He became a friend to my wife and me. I could feel his love and concern. His was truly the pure love of Christ in going after the one—not for statistics, but for my welfare.

My reactivation took several years. With my approval, missionaries came to teach my wife. I was happy to see her accept them, but I was afraid that if she decided not to join the Church, it might affect our marriage. So I played devil's advocate and dragged my feet the whole way. Only then could I be sure that when she decided to get baptized, it was for the testimony within her and not just to please me.

Another thing I worried about was that frequently missionaries were reassigned to other areas. I asked the Lord that if Sue were to accept the gospel, to please leave the senior companion in our area until her baptism. And that's exactly what happened. His name was Elder Chris Monson. He was humble and caring. It took him and his companions over nine months to teach Sue the gospel. He had companion after companion, but he remained until she was baptized.

While living in Chicago, I had finally become employed by an advertising typography shop called Design Typographers. I made a fair wage, first as a messenger, and then as a computer operator and repairman. The owner had two other shops in the suburbs where I also did repair work and cleaned their machines on weekends. This seemed satisfactory at first, but I began to long for a regular nine-to-five job Monday through Friday. I wanted and needed time off to be with my family and attend Church.

Fortunatley, I met the owner of a music store near my home. His name was Joseph Kupiszewski. He needed someone occasionally to help him move a grand piano that he rented out for concerts. Later on, he asked if I would like to become an apprentice piano technician rebuilding pianos. The pay again was good. And I could just about name my own hours. I really wanted to get back into music, anything in music. I began to train on weekends, then at home evenings. But then something went wrong. I'm not sure what; he never told me. He became angry one day, and the apprenticeship dissolved. In retrospect, I feel strongly that the Lord had his hand in this, making sure I went in another direction.

I still had my repair job, but I was disappointed. It was as if Heavenly Father wanted me to stay in the typesetting business. After this incident with Joe, I put all my effort into my repair job. I learned all aspects of the shop: camera, pasteup, proofing, keyboarding, and prgramming. Still, the boss would not agree to get me off the late nights and weekend work. I had made myself so indispensable that he felt he could not move me without disrupting the shop.

Then an amazing thing happened. While reading through a conference issue of the *Ensign* magazine one day, I noticed a problem that could only be made by the very typesetting machines I had learned to repair. I sent a letter to the *Ensign* letting them know that if they wanted me to tell them how to repair it, I would do so. My letter was forwarded to the Church typesetting department which was looking for a computer technician. They offered me a job. It was a tremendous cut in pay. But after Sue and I talked it over, we decided to move to Salt Lake City because we felt assured that was where the Lord wanted us.

I was hired by the church to repair four typesetting computers and two photoprocessors. But before the personnel department representatives could tell me I was accepted, I had to be interviewed by my bishop, Charles Smith, for temple worthiness. Everything seemed encouraging until the personnel representative wouldn't accept my bishop's answer. He kept asking questions about my past. Then one day Bishop Smith confided in me that he didn't think I was going to obtain the position. I recall telling him, "If the Lord wants me to work for the Church, I'll do it, and not the Personnel representative nor anyone else can stay the hand of the Lord, even if it takes years."

Within 24 hours, the personnel representative called and said, "The job is yours if you still want it." I told him I had to find a house in Utah before I could move and that I would get back with him. I then called a friend of mine from Ricks who lived in Granger, John Campbell, and expressly asked him to just get a newspaper at his convenience and look for a place for us. He agreed.

That was on Friday about 9:00 p.m. The next day he called me at 6:00 p.m. He said the strangest thing had happened. His wife's cousin had called after I had and said he was being transferred to Portugal for several years. He asked John if he knew anyone who would like to rent his house. The price he was asking was exactly the price I had told John I could pay.

We again felt the Lord's hand in helping us rent a house. The next hurdle was how to pay for our move. We had a yard sale. People bought items at such good prices that we could hardly believe it. Yet it wasn't enough money. Then my mother, still a nonmember of the Church, came to our rescue. She purchased our food storage, and with this we had enough to move to Utah.

The house we were to rent had not been vacated on time, so John and his wife, Chris, invited us to stay with them. Sue, our daughter Janessa, our two cats, and I lived and slept in one of their bedrooms for two weeks in ninety degree weather without air conditioning until our house was available.

Naturally, I had some problems at work at first, but I was able to handle them. Within seven months, I was promoted to output supervisor in charge of the very machines that I had repaired and supervising the people who operated them.

In the spring of 1983, my boss, Gene Smuin, asked me how music was printed in the United States today. He knew of my music education at Ricks and BYU and felt I was qualified to obtain such information. I called some industry leaders back East. Their consensus was that everyone was using the music typewriter, but that there was a music typeface for our typesetting computer. I told him I would try to put something together using it. He asked me to keep in touch and advise him if anything came of it.

I sat down at one of the computer terminals, and within an hour I was able to run out some staff lines and notes on it. Within a day or two, I had set an entire hymn, "Abide with Me." Because the song was on computer database, I next keyed in German words to the song as well as English. Mr. Smuin was impressed. He contacted his boss, and, as a result, the head of our department, Jim Mortimer, and the head of the music department, Michael Moody, arrived for a demonstration. The excitement mounted.

Brother Moody mentioned that the music committee had been waiting for something like this. He said that it was just the sort of thing that could pick up the momentum on the new hymnbook project that had been in limbo for some years.

Within a month, all the computer formats were in place to do the hymnbook. I sent samples to the man back East who had been so helpful when I was seeking information. He printed an article about our success in typesetting music. We even received letters in recognition of the music program from all parts of the USA, Canada, and as far away as Ireland.

However, it wasn't until March 30, 1984, that production actually began on the new hymnbook. It took fifteen months for four computer programmers and me to input and make corrections before the hymnbook was completed. The General Music Committee had between ten and twenty people proofing such items as key and time signatures, mood and metronome markings, note placement and spacing, word alignment and spelling, copyright information, composer and lyricist dates. There were also up to six pasteup artists in production until completion of the monumental project.

In celebration of the event, a hymnbook party was held in the Assembly Hall on Temple Square September 3, 1985. In attendance were General Authorities, composers, lyricists, committee members, and production people and spouses; in all almost 1,000 people. The Spirit was so evident that all of us felt love and thanksgiving.

Following this special occasion, a party was held in the South Visitors' Center where punch and goodies were served. Also, people signed our complimentary hymnbooks. Because the words written in mine have such deep meaning to me, I humbly share a few of them:

"It has been an honor to work with you on this project. We all know you were specially called to create the music for it and to lead the rest of us to completing it." —Sherry Bright (pasteup artist)

"I give you credit for much of the excitement and enthusiasm over the hymnbook—your work is perfect, and I have no doubt that the hand of Providence brought you here to do this work." —Michael Moody (Music Committee chairman and Music Department head)

"I really meant it when I said you were 'raised up for such a time as this.' I'm amazed at the complexity of your work and am awed at the beautiful results of your efforts . . . We'll all be grateful for it in the years to come as we sing these hymns. The Lord truly inspired you in this project." —Marvin Gardner (Music Committee member and editor)

Only part of what Randi Crookston (music programmer) wrote follows: "Words will not express all that I have felt this past year. When you started development of the music, I knew within my heart that I wanted to be involved. You, through the help of the Lord, have opened the way for more music to be published. I am grateful that I have had a small part of this wonderful historic 150th-year commemoration."

"This is a day which makes me so proud of you and thrilled to know what the Lord and you were able to do. You *HAD* to be a member of the church to produce this work of art. Love." —Darwin Wolford (Music Committee Member, editor, arranger, transcriber, missionary, and friend)

Since that time, much of the excitement has died down, but Sue and I now positively know why we moved to Utah and whose hand brought us. I had always prayed to be an instrument in the Lord's hand for good. I never thought it would be this rewarding in spirit. My only prayer is that I may live worthy to continue to assist in the building up of his kingdom on earth in preparation for his Second Coming, and that I may live to see him in glory and thank him face to face.

Randall J. (Randy) Nikola
West Valley City, Utah
July, 1987

A LIVING TESTIMONY

I would like to bear my testimony through an experience I am having. It started in February of 1969, just after I won the state championship in wrestling. The spirit of the devil had manipulated my pride, and I deceived myself by thinking no one or anything could hurt me. I had a "big head." Some of my close friends had tried to tell me, but I wouldn't listen. Even my seminary teacher talking to me made little difference. No one could reach me, and I began to let go of the iron rod. This is where the Lord stepped in. Our Heavenly Father has a mission for each of us, and mine had just begun.

On March 19 of the same year, while playing around in a high jump pit, I sustained a fractured neck in the fifth and sixth cervical vertebrae. It left me completely paralyzed from the neck down. I was immediately rushed to the Salt Lake LDS Hospital, where traction was prescribed. Elder Boyd K. Packer and a bishop from BYU gave me a blessing. I do not remember one word of the prayer, but I remember the peaceful and secure feeling at its conclusion. The doctors had told my parents that I would never walk or be able to button my own shirt again. I was never told this and always felt that the paralysis was only temporary.

After two operations and one and a half months in the LDS Hospital, I was moved to the University of Utah Hospital in Salt Lake for physical therapy. I regained all the functions of my limbs and eventually those of all my internal organs.

While I would never wish for anyone else to have a similar experience, it would be good if more people had the experience of learning to walk all over again. It would make them grateful that they can walk, run, think, see, and use all their senses. I believe people in general take these gifts from God for granted. A similar experience would help others become more aware of their environment and the miracle of bodies that function properly.

As well as being a physical strain, this experience has at times caused me embarrassment. Fear of the unknown causes more anxiety. It is easy to allow an evil spirit to tempt you to begin to wonder whether God is just.

I have learned that God has never let me down in any situation that was for my best good. He has already given me seventy-times-seven opportunities to grow, and he still blesses me every day.

It has been seventeen years since my accident, and I still limp. I cannot run and do a lot of the fun things that young men and women my age do. This has been hard on me mentally, but I have tried not to show my frustrations, and I have gotten by with the degree of mobility that has been restored. A good analogy is, "If you do not have a lot of food, you cannot eat much, but that does not mean you cannot make a good meal." While there are problems, I realize someone is always worse off than I.

I love life and love the God who gave it to me. To show my love, I made a covenant to serve God forever. Having served a mission to southern Texas, I am continuing in the service to repay my Heavenly Father for the miracle he performed through the priesthood on my behalf. Since serving my mission, I obtained a degree in teaching. Having taught in the public schools for five years, I now am a counselor in a school system. I have a beautiful wife, the former Carolyn Lambert, and we presently have one son, Daniel Blaine, which in itself is another miracle. Each day is an opportunity to learn and grow with the diverse experiences we face. The glory of God is intelligence. We cannot progress or gain exaltation unless we have a few hurdles to jump over. The Lord never puts anything in front of us that we cannot get over. Of course, he uses his own ways, not ours, and his ways are the best. I have in my heart the greatest gift ever given to me: I know God lives and that he loves me.

Steve Hawkes
August, 1986

A MOTHER SHARES HER FEELINGS

My son's junior year in high school started out a magic one for him. Steve decided he was going to take the state championship for his weight (148 pounds) in wrestling. Thinking he was dreaming too big, I told him it was good to set high goals but not to be too disappointed if he didn't win. He was determined; as the season went on, he proved he was serious. While we were praising him for winning matches, the Lord was preparing Steve for what was to happen, giving him something to recall during his long recovery. He took the district championship and won state, being the only contestant to pin all his opponents.

Steve had a sense of humor and was often the life of the party. He had six brothers and three sisters. His father was a bishop, his oldest brother was on a mission in Mexico, and another brother was in the army. Steve's wrestling matches were exciting for the whole family and drew us closer together.

When I returned from teaching school on March 19, 1969, just one month after Steve had won the State Championship, the children told me that Steve had been hurt. I was to go to the hospital immediately. Expecting a broken leg or something similar, I was shocked to find my son completely paralyzed from the neck down. While high jumping, he had landed directly on his head. The doctor looked very grave and called the LDS Hospital in Salt Lake City to arrange for Steve to go immediately. Before going Steve asked his father to give him a blessing, which he did. Leaving my husband, Blaine, home with the other children, I accompanied Steve in the ambulance.

After Dr. Stoops had checked Steve at the LDS Hospital, he and another doctor called me into a little room and told me that Steve would be just like he was then for the rest of his life. He said he needed permission to drill holes in Steve's skull so he could put traction on his neck. The spinal column had been injured, to what extent they could not say, but it could never repair itself. The traction would be to straighten the neck bone as much as possible. Steve's head was shaved. Two small holes were drilled into his outer skull and tongs were inserted in them. A wire with thirty pounds of weight was then connected to the tongs. Steve was put in intensive care on a Stryker frame and turned every two hours.

I spent a miserable night. I called Blaine to tell him what the doctors had told me. Dr. Barrott in St. Anthony had already told us the same thing. I stayed in the hospital all night, feeling that if I could just cry, some tension might be released. But tears would not come. I

never cried through the whole experience. Morning
came, and I could see Steve every hour. During the
middle of the morning, my sister, Betty, came to be with
me. She stayed several days. My brother, Terry, also came
and stayed with me. People were always dropping in. I
never realized that so many people from the St.
Anthony area went to Salt Lake every day. The day after
the accident, Steve's home teaching partner arrived with
a booklet from the Sugar City seminary students. They
had sat up all night preparing it to cheer Steve. One of
our dearest friends from Ashton called their son in Salt
Lake as soon as they heard of the accident, and he came
directly to see Steve. Blaine came to be with us over the
weekend. Friends from all over came to see us, and cards
and letters arrived every day.

Back home, people started sending food to our
home so fast that Blaine's mother filled the refrigerators
and freezers and had to call the Relief Society twice to ask
that people stop sending food. Then the Relief Society
organized a schedule so someone brought in a meal
every day for three weeks. By this time, I returned home.
After two days, I called to thank them and asked them to
discontinue sending food since I could prepare meals.

A special fast and prayer was held the night of the
accident. People of all ages from all over our town,
regardless of church affiliation, came and participated.
The Spirit of the Lord was so strong that no one wanted
to leave.

The seminary students immediately started a
"Cookie Jar of Fortune" for Steve. (Cookie was his
nickname.) By the end of the week, after a special dance,
they presented the family with over $500. The junior
class in Ashton that Steve had attended school with
earlier when we lived there, sent money. The PTA from
Parker, where I was teaching, had a cooked food sale for

us. Our brothers and sisters gave us money, and many other organizations and individuals donated money to help. This money paid for our traveling to Salt Lake each weekend, frequently bringing along some of Steve's friends with us. It also helped pay for Steve's phone calls home almost every night. We felt this played a big part in his recovery, helping him know his family and friends cared. It gave us all something to look forward to each night. Steve worked hard all day so he would have something new to tell us each night.

People were so kind that it is impossible to express adequate appreciation and the love we felt from them and for them.

A few days after being in the Salt Lake hospital with Steve, I asked Elder Boyd K. Packer to administer to him. He did not promise Steve that he would get well, but about a week after this blessing, he called to check on Steve. He said he had placed Steve's name on the prayer list for their General Authorities' meeting. He indicated that they were praying for him, and he felt Steve would be all right. Steve's name was also put on the prayer lists in the Idaho Falls, Logan, and Salt Lake temples.

Ten days after Steve's accident, the doctor operated on him to fuse the fifth and sixth vertebraes, entering from the front. They used animal bone from the bone bank to do the fusing. A special fast was held again at home. When the doctor came out of the operating room, he looked discouraged. He said he had literally removed hundreds of little pieces of shattered bone, and fused the fifth and sixth vertebraes. However, he was not pleased with the results of the operation. He said he would probably operate again the following Saturday.

The people at home fasted again. One little girl, too young to remember Steve's name, said in her prayers, "Please bless that boy we're all praying for."

By Thursday following the second operation, Steve's legs had started getting the sensation of being asleep which meant the feeling was starting to come back. The doctor told us we ought to go home and just visit him on weekends because he would get better faster without us there all the time. In another week, they were ready to put a full body cast on him, starting from the top of his head and leaving the top of the head open so that the holes would heal, his ears and face out, and ending down below his hips so that he couldn't sit up straight on a chair. The next few nights were probably the most miserable of the whole ordeal for him, as he tried to get used to being locked up so tightly.

The day Steve got his cast, fourteen of his schoolmates came to see him. They had a ball out in the hall, and even Dr. Stoops joined in the fun. His friends left so he could rest and then returned later to say good-bye. Each was sobered by Steve's cheerfulness. He was so happy to see them. I was grateful to the parents for allowing their young people to make this long trip to cheer him. Steve maintained this attitude the whole time he was in the hospitals.

He was in the university Hospital for rehabilitation. Here he worked hard and even helped cheer up other patients. Little by little, he learned to use his hands again. How happy I was on Mother's Day to receive a gift card written in his own small, neat handwriting—"To my dear mother, from Steve."

He learned to walk and crawl, all with the cast on. He was two inches taller but very thin. On August 15 he was finally released to come home! What a happy day to see him walk up our stairs with his cane. The doctors advised him to use a wheelchair in school to prevent any accident. One of his friends followed him around for a week with the wheelchair, but Steve refused to use it. By the end of October, he had thrown his cane away.

Just before Steve came home, Dr. Stoops came to the University Hospital to see him. "Well," he said, "I never would have believed it. Steve, you made a liar out of me, but I don't mind at all. I honestly didn't believe you could do it, but I am happy you did."

Today Steve still has a definite limp, and his left side isn't as good as his right one, but he can do small intricate work very neatly. The Lord has blessed him, and his health keeps improving. He filled a mission to the Texas South Mission, and, as his patriarchal blessing says, he is "a living witness to the divinity of the power, mercy, and goodness of the Lord."

This experience has been a joy to me in more ways than one. While I'm not happy that Steve had to go through this and that he is handicapped, the testimony and blessings we have all received from it are miracles in themselves. The Lord blessed us with a willingness to accept Steve's misfortune in his life and ours. I have a testimony of the Lord's answer to prayers and of the importance and value of fasting. Also, the Lord has strengthened the testimonies of many young people due to his experience.

I know the Lord loves us very much. I know that he loves Steve very much and that he didn't prevent the accident from happening in order to help him stay a good person. Our family has a great appreciation for all the love and concern of our relatives and friends.

Bonnie Clark Hawkes
August, 1986

OUR MIRACLE BABY

Some of our most difficult and painful experiences help us grow the most. Having a seriously ill, premature baby blessed and taught us.

David and I were married in January, 1977. In October of that year, we had our first child, a daughter, whom we named Corriann. We enjoyed her even through colic and first-time parenting trials. She's a special girl and patient with our practicing on her.

We hoped to have a large family, and since we were both twenty-six when we married, we didn't want to wait long for our second baby. That wasn't the Lord's plan for us though. After almost four years of going to doctors, praying, fasting, and waiting, we still had not been blessed with another child. As we prayed, we decided to pursue adoption. We really wanted Corriann to learn and grow by having brothers and sisters.

We filled out all the forms, took the physicals, had the interviews, and eventually received a letter accepting us as an adoptive family. The agency indicated that it would take from eighteen months to two years to get our baby. It was hard to believe we were finally going to have another baby. About a year after we had been accepted, I called the people at the agency with the news that the Lord had decided to send our baby direct. They were happy for us and said they would keep our name on the list just in case we had problems.

The months we waited were special. I experienced the usual morning sickness but also a wonderful excitement. I had some quiet spiritual times. Corriann went to kindergarten each day at noon, and I had time alone. I rested, prayed, and read scriptures. I feel this daily devotional helped prepare me for the difficult times ahead. I went into the birth of our second child, Ellie Jean, and the complications that followed with a "full lamp." I was spiritually prepared, and what a great blessing that was. Also, we were better prepared temporally than we ever were before or since. I had put a good stock of food and household items away. When the time came, I was able to use grocery money for travel to be with Ellie. I know why Church leaders continually encourage us to be prepared. Following their counsel blessed us.

On Saturday, May 7, 1983, things began to go really wrong in my formerly normal pregnancy. I experienced a good deal of pain periodically and felt generally miserable. The next day was Mother's Day, and I attended all the church meetings. As counselor in the Relief Society, I conducted that Sunday. By the time meetings were over on Sunday morning I was in a lot of pain, but I didn't want to admit I was in labor at only six months. I called the doctor who assumed my problem was a bladder infection. David and Corriann went for a prescription. By the time they returned, I knew the problem was much more serious than that. I called the doctor again, and we were soon on our way to Madison Memorial Hospital in Rexburg, leaving Corriann with her aunt.

Another word of counsel from Church leaders blessed us at this time—stay close to your extended family. Because of the nature of my transfer from Rexburg, Idaho, to the university Medical Center at Salt

Lake City, Utah, by ambulance, plane, and helicopter, David was unable to go with me. As soon as I left, he went home and called my aunt, a lady I love dearly, who lives near Salt Lake. When I arrived at the hospital in Salt Lake, she, my uncle, and a cousin were waiting for me. She held my hand while Ellie was being born, and my uncle and David placed their finger tips on Ellie's tiny head and administered to her. David had made the long five-hour drive through the night alone, arriving shortly after Ellie was born. He and my brother-in-law had administered to me before I left Rexburg.

We had shared with members of our ward both our desire to have more chidren and our joy at my being pregnant. As the news of our problem became known, ward members began praying for us. On Monday they held a ward fast and that evening met briefly at the church for a prayer together in our behalf. We felt their love two hundred and fifty miles away in a hospital room and intensive-care nursery in Salt Lake.

Ellie Jean was born at 12:45 a.m. that Monday. She weighed only two pounds and two ounce, fourteen and one-half inches tall, and was in critical condition, unable to breathe on her own, eat, or even maintain her body temperature. Her life was totally supported by machines and those prayers. All that could be done was done for her.

I believe that when a child is born, the veil is often very thin. This was the case when Ellie was born. The first time I saw her was when they wheeled me into the intensive care unit at the hospital. To me she was beautiful even with all the machinery and a breathing tube in her mouth and throat. She was struggling, unable to cry because of the tubes. She squeezed my little finger in her tiny hand. I felt she was communicating with someone on the other side, "This is too hard; I can't do it. Please let me come back where it is warm and safe," and He was answering, "Oh, yes! Life is hard, but it is worth it. You can only know true joy when you have experienced pain." The feeling came to me that this tiny little baby girl would someday be a mother and experience the pain and joy of giving birth. The thought comforted me during the following weeks when her progress was slow and she seemed to be taking two steps backward for each step forward. I wondered if she would ever breathe on her own, eat, or grow and be a normal baby.

On Monday after visiting Ellie in the nursery, we felt strongly that our tiny little daughter needed something more to be known by than Baby Atkinson. We decided on the name Ellie Jean. It was one of the names we had discussed earlier, and it felt just right. With so much love and support from our ward members, we felt she was theirs as much as ours, and we decided to wait until she was healthy enough to attend a fast and testimony meeting in our ward to receive her name and a blessing. We had faith that she would live to see that time, and we knew that if Heavenly Father decided to take her home before then, her name could still be placed on the church records of the Church. Since she was born in the covenant, we knew she would be ours forever according to our faithfulness.

During the days and weeks after her birth, my consuming concern was for her. I went home to St. Anthony, Idaho, for about four days the week after she was born. The hospital called us every other day to let us know how she was doing. I lived in anxiety waiting for the calls, and they never seemed quite satisfying. Our home seemed empty without her even though she had never been there after she was born. I had felt her presence with me, and her absence was obvious when I came home without her.

We finally decided I needed to be with her, and she seemed to do better when I was there. Though there wasn't a physical thing that could be done for her that wasn't being done by the nurses, my presence seemed to help. Being there, talking to the doctors, other parents, and friends seemed to really help me.

The people at the University Medical Center were very kind and understanding. Even with all the machinery and the urgency of the work in the newborn intensive care unit, they tried to create a warm atmosphere with rocking chairs and soft music. They allowed the families to bring little toys and pictures. They also permitted brothers and sisters to scrub down and wear special little gowns so they could see and even hold the hand of a new, very sick brother or sister. This was a special experience for Corriann and helped her love Ellie and understand more about what was taking place.

When her skin was no longer too tender to touch, a kind nurse let me help her find a tiny dress among those donated by parents, and we dressed her for the first time. I appreciated that extra kindness and so many others shown us by doctors and nurses and others who seemed to understand what we were experiencing.

For the first month I spent the majority of my time in Utah staying with a cousin and his wife who opened their home and hearts to me. I spent most of my days at the hospital by Ellie's isolette as long as was good for her and in the lobby and parents' room, writing, talking, and praying. My heart rose and fell many times during those weeks. She developed blood clots, a heart murmur, intestinal infection, pneumonia, and lost about three more ounces. It appeared for a while that she had suffered some brain damage at birth. (The blood that appeared in an ultrasound of her head later cleared away, and she was pronounced completely normal.)

I went to the Jordan River and Salt Lake temples a few times during that period and found great peace and solace therein. On one occasion, I knelt and prayed. Ellie was having a hard time, but I received a sure answer to my prayers, "You know she is going to live. I told you when she was born. Lift up your heart and trust me." After that I was able to go home and be at peace. I visited her a couple of weekends when I got a ride, and then she was transferred to Bannock Memorial Hospital at Pocatello, Idaho. There she was just two hours from home, and we could see her more often.

The first month of Ellie's life was a difficult one for David. His calm, quiet life was suddenly torn apart. He didn't feel the closeness to Ellie that I had. The responsibility of running the household fell on his shoulders. He also faced the extremely frightening prospect of astronomical medical bills. It has always been his nature and within his power to pay our obligations when due, and we've always made careful decisions and planned carefully before taking on new obligations. We had medical insurance, but we had never tested it in a crisis situation. It took time for the insurance company to process the myriad of claims that were sent in regularly. Meanwhile, at home David was receiving unpleasant letters and threats from billing companies, doctors, and hospitals. He meticulously checked and rechecked the bills and claims. I helped figure out who they were from and what they were for. In the end, the insurance company paid all but $2,000 of bills that came to nearly $90,000. We worked that out and paid our part by the time all the paperwork was done. The anxiety of not knowing and not quite trusting the insurance company's willingness to live up to its commitment caused us much apprehension and concern. So often we worry and fret when the ball is in the other fellow's court and we can do nothing but wait.

Finally Ellie was transferred to Rexburg, Idaho, just twelve miles from home. By then I had complete confidence she would be all right. She was now free form machinery except for the incubator to keep her warm. She still needed special help with feeding sometime, but we could visit her twice a day. Corriann sat outside the nursery, watching through the window, as David and I went into play with and feed Ellie. We were proud of Corriann's patience and willingness to open her heart to Ellie. She had been the center of our lives, and suddenly I was gone. She spent her days with Grandma Bonnie Atkinson or in outside nurseries alone while our attention was lavished on Ellie. She seemed to grow to love Ellie as much as we did. When Ellie was born, we told Corri she weighed just as much as two pounds of butter, and the nurse sent home a little preemie diaper so she could see it. She took it to kindergarten for Show and Tell, and, being quite shy, she simply held the diaper up in front of the class and said, "Two pounds of butter."

In kindergarten she drew a picture of her family showing herself, David, and me, holding a little baby in my arms. It touched me deeply because at that time I had not been able to hold Ellie in my arms. I took that picture back to the hospital in Salt Lake, and we taped it on Ellie's isolette so she would know Corriann.

The day did come, and we were that family carrying our little baby out of the hospital. It was August 3, 1983 (my due date), and a wonderful day in our memory. She weighed four pounds two ounces, double her birth weight.

On September 4, 1983, when Ellie Jean was almost five months old she attended her first church meeting, a fast and testimony meeting. There with many of the people who had prayed fervently in her behalf, she received her name and a father's blessing from her dad, assisted by Grandpa Atkinson, Grandpa Baker, an uncle, and the bishopric.

Since Ellie's birth, David, Corriann, and I attended at least sacrament meeting every Sunday. When I was in Utah, I went with the relatives with whom I stayed. At home I went to our ward until Ellie came home to stay and we were advised not to take her in crowds. I was released from my Relief Society calling, but David continued serving as elders quorum president. He went to our ward and came home to take care of Ellie while I attended sacrament meeting in another ward at a different time. I knew the Lord had blessed us in preserving her life, and I wanted to do all I could to show my love and commitment to him. I shared my testimony and received the blessings of partaking of the sacrament and feeling others' testimonies.

We have certainly grown as a family through this experience. It has brought us closer to our Heavenly Father and to our fellowmen who suffer trials. We have come to know how precious and sacred life is, and we have made a stronger commitment to live the gospel, to follow the counsel of our leaders, and to help our fellowmen.

Today Ellie Jean is a healthy, strong, normal three-year-old. She has no further medical problems and is a joy to our family.

Colleen (Cody) Baker Atkinson
September 11, 1986

Compiler's note: On April 24, 1987, Cody and David were blessed with a baby son whom they named Steven. However, the nurses and doctors at the Madison Memorial Hospital remembered little Ellie and referred to Steven as "Ellie's baby brother."

BE THE BEST YOU CAN BE

I was born and raised in Salt Lake City. Although we were brought up in a meager home, my parents and brothers and sister are such fine people that I now know we were richer and more blessed than persons deserve to be in this life. Like Nephi of old, I was born of goodly parents—the third of their seven children. My father was bishop of our ward when I was born and has served in almost every priesthood leadership position since that time. Mother is an earthly angel who loves and happily sustains and supports her husband in whatever he is called to do. She is a positive and contented woman, happy to have children and raise them up to love and serve their Heavenly Father. Mother has met many difficult challenges and is a wonderful example of womanhood. I consider my parents and family one of the best things that has happened to me in this life.

I graduated from Brigham Young University in physical education in 1964. I taught one year at San Juan High School in Blanding, Utah; three years at West High School in Salt Lake City; and two years at Madrone Intermediate School in northern California before joining the faculty of Ricks College in 1970.

As a young girl, I did not realize I would be single so much of my life. I am so thankful that I obtained an education. This has opened many doors for me and given me the opportunity to work as I have chosen to do. I enjoy teaching and have been blessed to love to go to work each day. There are always students waiting to learn, and I know I can teach them.

I have found that as I take the opportunity to qualify myself in anything, those newly learned qualifications open new doors in my life. This has made my life full and challenging. I earned my Young Women's Campcrafter certification from the General Board one year when it was offered. I took a day's leave from West High School without pay to complete the certification, and within two weeks, I was called as a stake camp director. I took Lifesaving and Water Safety Instructor's training when I lived in California because it was offered free through Red Cross, and I had always wanted to swim correctly. In only a few weeks I signed a contract to teach swimming and other sports at Ricks College. After the Teton Dam flood, I began taking nursing classes while I was teaching, so I would never be "just another mouth to feed" in times of need. Now I work summers as a registered nurse wherever I choose to live. I have learned that if you prepare yourself, opportunities that will be best for you open up.

Nearly four years ago while I was coaching and teaching at Ricks, I was called to serve a mission for the Church. I was surprised because I was teaching, coaching two sports, buying a trailer, etc. My bishop said, "Do as you wish, but the Lord wants you to serve a mission."

I was given a leave of absence from Ricks, and my parents were thrilled to support me. I was fortunate to serve fifteen months in England. I learned to respect all that my pioneer ancestors had given up so I could live in this lovely free country of America. I worked hard to be the best missionary I could be, so I would never have to wonder why I hadn't done my best by every interested person. Those were wonderful months.

I have been blessed to be able to do my best in whatever came my way and not to concern myself unduly with what did not come my way. I honestly believe that each person, each woman, must strive and pray to be productive and content and to serve happily wherever she is today. Being married or single is not what brings true joy. We must always realize our true worth and potential and do as much as we possibly can to develop that potential. All women have talents and gifts to share. When they are united in a righteous cause, the Lord blesses them with the strength of love and true concern for their fellowmen. In the Relief Society where I now serve, I can see how every talent is needed to make the ward strong and effective.

My teams have won national championships and have done temple work together in temples around the land. We have attended funerals and baptisms together, and we have laughed and had fun. We make our own opportunities. I know that God knows us and truly cares about what we are doing in our lives of service for him.

My patriarchal blessing says that I will look back through the stream of time and know that my Heavenly Father has guided me in every walk of life. I trust that Heavenly Father knows what is best for me in my life and for each of you as well. Do not lament that you have not but build up the individual that you are. We must prepare ourselves to live with God by becoming like him. President Benson said that the measure of true greatness is how close we can become like Jesus, that that person is greatest who is most Christlike, and that those who love him most will be most like him.

Many individuals, married and single, do not realize how many people their lives affect and touch or how much good they can be to any with whom they associate. One year as I was teaching in Salt Lake City, I saw this fact clearly demonstrated. I was living at home with my family. My grandmother lived across the street, and what a blessing she was in our lives! After a day of teaching, I would go visit with her and have a couple of salty pickles from the crock. (They were delicious!) One day as I walked through her yard, I noticed a small neighbor girl doing handstands against her garage. She was there the next day, too. I soon found myself shouting suggestions to her to help her with the skills. Then I went over in the yard to spot and teach. Before long we had a standing appointment most evenings to practice together. I taught her cheers and flips. For the homecoming celebration at West High that year, her mom bought her a red and black outfit and allowed Monica to come to school one day with me. Monica led our eighty-member Pep Club in a few cheers. The girls loved her, and Monica was thrilled.

About six years passed, and we lost touch with one another. I received a call from Monica one night while I was teaching in California. She thought I would like to know she had taken second place in the the high school gymnastics meet. I did want to know. I was thrilled! I was also delighted a few years later when she married a fine young man in the temple of God. None of her five sisters had chosen temple marriages. I know it takes many positive influences in a life to guide a young person to be worthy of temple marriage. Those years of sports participation that followed our association were definitely positive factors in Monica's life.

Another such experience occurred when I was teaching and coaching at Ricks. I was a campus Relief Society president, taking classes toward my nursing degree. As I came to my office one morning, I found a card under my door. It was signed "a friend," and it said, "Because of you, I am able to go on!" I did not know who could possibly be leaning on me for strength to go on. I had to sit down at my desk for lack of strength. I found myself treating everyone I knew just a little better, just in case they might be the one relying on me.

It does matter how we live. People are watching and counting on each of us. They know basically how Mormons should live, and they watch carefully to see if we are following that lifestyle. We can be an example to all we work and associate with.

These are some experiences of my life that have helped make the years meaningful and rich. I am truly a blessed person. I have only had two goals to guide my life: (1) To always do my best, and (2) to be a good girl. These are still my goals. I have added one more such goal these past years, and that is to be happy being a good girl while striving to do my best. I do enjoy life and all I am doing. I was asked a few months ago which of my Church callings has been my favorite. My reply was easy: "The one I have now as Relief Society president." It is such a fine opprotunity to know and serve the women of the ward. Before I began serving in this calling, I determined to enjoy it while the carnivals, board meetings, and service opportunities were in full progress. I am enjoying myself very much. Throughout my life, I have found that the Lord guides and blesses the lives of those who truly seek him in service to others.

I pray that I may always have the ability to remain true and to serve my Heavenly Father so I will feel the self-worth, inner joy, and contentment that we each seek so earnestly. I know that this Church is true. It means more to me than life itself. I know my Heavenly Father cares for me and guides my eternal steps back toward him as he does each one of his children.

JoAnn Reeve

MIRACLES DO HAPPEN

It had been warm in the Idaho Falls Temple that December 9 evening, 1983. It was not only warm from the furnace but also from the warmth of fellowship and love from those who come each week to serve someone who has passed on and cannot personally say, "Thank you."

Attending the temple is truly the highlight of my week since my husband, Burdette, died nineteen years ago. It allows me to serve and receive spiritual strength for the week ahead. I had paid special attention to the prayer that was said that night in the temple, asking the Lord to bless those who must travel long distances that they may return safely to their homes. I needed assurance that God was mindful of me as I traveled ten miles alone to Parker, Idaho, after leaving my friends in Rexburg.

After completing our assignments for the evening, we prepared to leave the temple. As we opened the door, the chill air took our breath away. We hurried to our car, walking very carefully on the icy walks and steps.

Fern Ricks, Rula Hinckley, and I were widows and enjoyed our association. For several years, we had shared the carpool from Rexburg to Idaho Falls, a distance of thirty miles. The freeway was usually clear from snow and ice and caused us little worry. On our way home this particular night, we talked of how blessed we were to be privileged to come each week and partake of the blessing of officiating in the House of the Lord.

The country road to Parker had little travel and was extremely icy this night. Fern urged me to stay all night with her, but ten miles didn't seem very far, and I assured her I would drive carefully and slowly, and all would be fine. After all, hadn't I driven that same road every week for four years and nothing had ever happened. "Call me when you arrive home then," she said, "so I will be able to sleep."

It took awhile for the defroster to clear the ice crystals from my windshield, but soon the car began to warm, and I was on my way toward Parker. All went well until I came to the county line between Madison and Fremont. As I went through the intersection, my car hit an icy rut, sending it out of control.

I tried to think quickly what I had read to do in such a situation, but the car was in a spin and I was too frightened to respond properly. The car skidded to the other side of the road and went backwards into a four-foot-deep snow bank.

At last it came to an abrupt stop off the road, its back end buried in snow left by a snow plow.

I sat there in shock listening to my pounding heart. I finally let loose my grip of the steering wheel and looked in both directions to see if a car might be coming. I felt a bit relieved when I considered that I might have gone into the spin as I was approaching another car. It could have been tragic. Amazingly, I was not hurt and soon commenced to assess my predicament. It was too cold for me to leave the car to go for help; besides there was not a light in any of the homes I had passed. Most people in the country are asleep at 11:30 p.m.

I knew it was subzero weather by the radio weather report. If I left the car running, I could become sleepy and be asphyixiated or run out of gas before help arrived. If I tried to start the car and drive out, I might sink farther and farther into the drift.

I realized it was hopeless to clear myself. My only answer was to turn to a power greater than mine. From the time I was a little girl in the home of my loving parents, Sidney and Martha Hanks, I had been taught to believe in prayer, and I had had many prayers answered. I said simply, "Lord, please help me. Help me to know what to do." Still there were no cars coming in either direction.

As if a voice spoke to me, I was prompted to start the car and to put it into gear. Very carefully I applied the gas; then came the miracle! The car began to move forward as if several men were pushing it. The wheels didn't spin or sink into the soft snow; they moved ahead ever so slowly but surely. I could not believe what was happening. When at last I was on the road, I was facing the wrong way. I went back to the corner where the car had started skidding, slowly turned around, and headed for home. I did not cry or tremble, but I felt a sweet peace and calm feeling that told me everything was going to be all right. It seemed as if someone were sitting in the seat beside me.

As I turned into my driveway at home, I touched the garage door button, and the door went up. The fervent prayer at the temple had most assuredly been answered in my behalf. It was then that my tears fell hot on my cheeks as I breathed a prayer of gratitude to my Heavenly Father for his protecting care and my safe return to the security of my home.

I hadn't planned to relate this experience to anyone, not even to my own family. I felt they would tell me I was driving too fast. However, the next morning when I saw that the side of my car was caved in on the driver's side, I *knew* that guardian angels had been my companions that night. They knew what help I needed and supplied it.

I know that on my own I am nothing, but with sincere prayer and trust in my Heavenly Father nothing is impossible. I am reminded of this scripture: "Be thou humble; and the Lord thy God shall lead thee by the hand, and give thee answer to thy prayers." (D&C 112:10.)

Martha Hanks Remington
June, 1984

A MORMON MIRACLE

Being a recipient of miracles is not new to me. Limited space warrants sharing only one incident. It occurred in October, 1983, in Morgan Hill, California. My daughter, Jodi, and our dear neighbor, Diane Milburn, insisted on taking me to the Santa Teresa Hospital in San Jose on October 3. I had suffered for three weeks with severe stomach pains. I couldn't even drink water due to the pain it caused. I feared going but feared not going more.

When I was admitted, I had started to dehydrate and my temperature was 102 degrees. IV's were immediately started; then came X-rays followed by a nasal pharnyx tube (one through the nose to the stomach). My stomach was continually pumped and waste fluids went up a tube into a container at the head of the bed. The fluid began to be a bright red and continued thus for six days.

Huge spots covered my entire body. My whole hand was one spot; arms, legs, body, and face were swollen and covered with saucer-size spots raised about an inch in some areas, one-half inch in others. My bloated body looked grotesque. With tubes everywhere, I was a sight, a sight I've preferred to forget; yet it's important to remember.

That Friday night the doctor told my husband, Dave, he didn't believe I would survive the weekend. I became so swollen that I couldn't bend my fingers; my eyes were mere slits, and my glasses didn't fit. Itching and burning made me feel like I was on fire; my temperature continued to rise.

The doctors were baffled as the tube continued to flow with my blood. I had every available test, yet they couldn't determine what caused the swelling or the bleeding. They decided the swelling could be from an unknown virus. The bleeding was their most disturbing problem.

My blood count steadily dropped. In one day's time it dropped below half of what it should have been. I was terribly frightened. I could see the blood in the tube and realized there were no answers at least it seemed that way.

Dave called on Saturday after a week of having no answers from the doctors. I said, "Please find someone to come and help you give me a priesthood blessing." Dave was working out of town and unable to come until Sunday. A Brother Rodriquez anointed my head, and Dave pronounced the blessing. I was dopey and weak but recall that he asked our Heavenly Father to ease my pain and stop the bleeding. Within ten minutes, the first blood transfusion was started, and the pain had eased in a most amazing way. I didn't feel any discomfort.

At two a.m. I was awakened by a strange burning sensation in my stomach. It was not painful, just burning. A nurse was starting my next transfusion. I mentioned this to her. She suggested giving me medication for pain, but I assured her that wasn't necessary, that I only had a very strange firey feeling. Later that morning there was not a drop of red in the NG tube! It appeared clear or pale yellow, like normal gastric juices. A specialist examined me through a tube. He was amazed at the evidence of pits. He told me they must have been sores and had caused the bleeding, that my whole stomach looked scorched or seared, similar to after a fire. My internal wounds had actually been cauterized. All was normal except he said he had never seen a stomach lining that looked like mine. His report brought relief immediately.

Knowing I was a Mormon (and he wasn't), he said, "I guess you'll call this one of your Mormon miracles, won't you?" I smiled and nodded because that is what it was. I was not astonished at what he had seen. I had felt the fire and had witnessed that the blood flow had ceased. I knew the doctors helped me, but it was Heavenly Father who had answered our prayers. I had been healed through the power of his priesthood.

I am grateful my husband was able to help bless me and that the Lord performed this miracle. My case was a rare study for the doctors.

I know the Lord loves me and honors my prayers. I will continue to testify of the power of his priesthood and of his watchful care. He blesses me even when I am least deserving. I love him and desire to do his will. I humbly thank him for our three children, Jodi, John, and James, that I am a mother in Zion and a Latter-day Saint. I know God loved the world enough to give his only begotten Son, Jesus Christ, to atone for everyone's sins and that whoever believes in our Redeemer, accepts his atonement, and abides by his teachings shall receive immortality and eternal life.

Deanne Ernst Allen
October, 1985

MY FEELINGS FOR LIFE

As is written in 1 Nephi, 1:2, I, too, was born of goodly parents, Anthony and Crystal Gardner, on October 15, 1955.

My birth, early that morning, turned out to be a little different than they anticipated. I had several broken bones and seemed to be extremely fragile. Several days later, my parents took me to Salt Lake City for examination and treatment. They were hopeful that the doctors would be able to tell them all about my physical problem, how I got it, and what could be done in my behalf.

After a couple of weeks at the hospital there, they were informed that the doctors still were not really sure what my problem was or what had caused it. They knew that it was not hereditary, that I was very fragile, and that my bones would break easily. They advised my parents that it probably would be best for all concerned if they put me in a facility where I could have the constant medical care that would be necessary the rest of my life to meet my special needs.

However, because I was born of goodly parents, they loved me enough not to take the easy way out. Instead, they took me home to St. Anthony, Idaho, to meet the rest of the family—four sisters: Wana, Sharla, Toni, and Kristine; and one brother, Kim. They left Salt Lake knowing that the road ahead of us would be long, hard, full of trials and problems but knowing that together and with the blessings of our loving Heavenly Father we would make it.

My childhood years were extra special, and even though I was often watching the games and other children playing from a hospital bed because of another broken bone, I still enjoyed many good times with lots of good friends.

When time to start grade school finally came, Mother or Dad carried me to school and then put me in my wheelchair since I still hadn't learned to walk.

I had attempted to walk when I was four with the help of braces and crutches. We were thrilled when I was able to go on my own. The joy was short-lived, however, because soon my muscles were stronger than my bones, and I began to suffer severe muscle spasms which in turn broke bones in my legs. The dream of walking then, or ever, began to seem impossible; we started to believe that what the doctors had told us could be true—that I would probably never be able to walk.

When I was 11, we made another trip to Salt Lake to see a new doctor, Sherman S. Coleman. When we arrived, he took one look at me, and said, "When can you be here to have surgery so you can start learning to walk, young lady?"

After the shock of his question wore off, he told us I was suffering from a rare disease known as osteogenesis imperfecta. Not until then had we known a name for my problem. We told him we would be back on February 21, 1966, for the first of several operations he planned to perform on my legs to strengthen them to support my body weight. The procedure involved cutting the bones in my legs into small pieces and inserting steel rods up through the bone to provide the strength and support I needed.

After three surgeries and a lot of time in casts and bed, I got my first pair of braces and crutches and slowly learned the art of balance and walking. It was a great and exciting day for me and my family—a dream come true! Up to that point in my life, I had suffered somewhere between 50 and 100 broken bones.

As an example of how fragile my bones really were, one time as I was playing with some friends, one of them playfully grabbed a toy from my hand, breaking my arm. Another time, a small child's chair tipped over across my legs, breaking both of them. On another occasion as we were driving down the road in the car, I turned to look into the back seat and the big tibia bone in one of my legs snapped. It was a nerve-wracking way to live. No one ever knew when such incidents would next occur, including me. We all learned to take one day at a time and to be very careful. Since those surgeries, I have not had any broken bones, although I still am cautious. Also, because of the many broken bones I had when I was younger, I did not grow normally, so I am only four feet tall, another great challenge I have had to learn with and to overcome.

I am now 28 years old and have graduated from high school and junior college. I have my own home, drive my own car, and hold a full-time job. These things have come quite easily for me. I enjoyed school and did well in most subjects. I had a lot of friends who made my school days fun and exciting and who helped me immensely. I have had several jobs which I enjoyed, and I have found that regardless of physical handicaps, people will trust you to work for them if you do your part and prove to them that you are a normal person inside and can carry your share of the workload. I have been grateful for the many employers who have given me the opprotunity to prove myself.

My life has been full of good times and lots of happy memories. Things have not always been easy and sometimes, naturally, I have wondered why it all happened to me and why I have had to suffer. I have taken great comfort in my testimony of the gospel of Jesus Christ and have often read my patriarchal blessing which says that some of the Lord's choicest spirits are being tried in the crucible of fire. The Lord has said he will have a tried people and some of his leaders and choice children are those who ofttimes are tested the most. I like to think that I am one of his choice children and have always tried to do what I think he would have me do.

I have been privileged to hold many Church callings and am presently serving as first counselor in the St. Anthony Fourth Ward Primary. To have a calling like this has been an inspiration to me. I have felt the Lord's hand in many of the plans and decisions we have made as a presidency, and I feel especially blessed to serve in this humbling position. It is true that the Lord will not try us beyond what we are able to handle. At times when I have felt sorry for myself and been discouraged, something always happens to make me appreciate what I do have, why I am able to do what I do, and I am made aware that my life is easier, more meaningful, and happy because of my family and friends.

One scripture in D&C 121:7-9 sums up my feelings about my life and life in general: "My son, peace be unto thy soul; thine adversity and thine afflictions shall be but a small moment;

"And then, if thou endure it well, God shall exalt thee on high; thou shalt triumph over all thy foes.

"Thy friends do stand by thee, and they shall hail thee again with warm hearts and friendly hands."

The following poem also sums up my life and the feelings I have for life.

From quiet homes and first beginnings
Out to the undiscovered ends.
There's nothing worth the wear of living,
But laughter, and love, and friends.

Konie Gardner
January, 1983

ADVERSITY AND TRIAL

I am the fifth child of a family of nine born to Raymond and Opal Whittier. My father had a great beginning in his venture into the business world. In 1920, the year of my birth, owning an automobile was becoming the dream of every American family. My father saw the opportunity to become a Dodge dealer, so he and a neighbor rented a small building in Delco, Idaho.

The business was very successful. My parent's home expanded from a small house with a kitchen, dining room, and one bedroom to one with an additional bedroom, pantry, upstairs, and a full basement for the childrens' sleeping quarters. We felt very blessed.

Then came 1928, the year the great depression hit. My father's business had expanded from this small garage in Delco to a business interest in a dealership on Van Ness Avenue in San Francisco, California. In the span of a few days in October, 1928, what had been a promising business turned into a nightmare with the closure of the banks.

Things had been going so well for my father that he had not noticed the troublesome signs in our economy. He had complete faith in the banking system and, as a result, had not diversified his investments. When the stock market crashed and the banks closed their doors, our family was left penniless with only mortgages to pay off and no access to the liquid assets my parents had so frugally and carefully accumulated in banking institutions.

My father, who was then a bishop, was so despondent that I heard him talk about going out and having an accident so my mother could collect a one-thousand-dollar life insurance policy. The sheriff removed all our household belongings. We spent days and nights eating and sleeping on the floors while our parents managed a farm that had been foreclosed on by a Utah mortgage company.

Mother was always a pillar of strength. She and Father now had seven children. When he suggested collecting on the life insurance policy, she became so angry that she tore it up. This action seemed to breed strength and determination into the whole family's goals.

We started having family counsel gatherings. Inspirational messages given to the small children in the family were indelibly impressed on my mind and became the saving principles of my future life.

I remember my parents telling me, "People are not very impressed with the starts we make; what everybody wants to know is how we finish. We cannot live in those grandious upper rooms that life has set aside for our occupancy if we abandon our goals in life because of momentary hardships or setbacks. If, because we are faced with hardship, we cast aside our goals and our dreams, these magnificent rooms of our possibilities may go eternally unfinished and unoccupied. The most serious shortcomings of our existence are not our intentional transgressions but our inability to finish what we start."

Although I didn't realize it at the time, this truth became a beacon on the spiritual and intellectual geography of my whole existence.

Because of the humble circumstances our family was remanded to as a result of the Great Depression, I made up my mind that I was going to get an education, preparing myself for an occupation that no bank or lending institution could foreclose on and take away from me. I was aware that because of the large number of children in our family, my parents would not be able to help me financially.

This reality opened up new horizons to me. Instead of waiting for some opportunity to come along, I began looking into opportunities that others had experienced difficulties with and thus abandoned.

I noticed that during the sugar beet growing season their leaves often turned yellow and developed holes, even though there was an abundance of fertile soil and water.

One letter to the Department of Agriculture division of entomology inquiring about this phenomenon made the financing of my college education possible. The discoloration and deterioration of the sugar beet leaf was caused by a leaf hopper called ute tix tenelis bake. It was extremely small; its breeding habit and life style were surrounded by mystery.

Even though I was only a sophomore in high school, because I took the time to inquire about this tiny insect, an entomologist at the Department of Agriculture Experiment Station in Twin Falls, Idaho, became interested. He offered to pay me $75.00 per month to come to his laboratory and study and work with him to uncover the mysteries of this environmental affliction. To help you appreciate the magnitude of this opportunity, my father was working with a team and wagon for $2.00 per day.

This opportunity to work had been offered to others but because it involved tiny insects, long, tiring hours of work, and frequent failures, they abandoned the studies and went to easier tasks. The study resulted in assisting the development of a disease resistant species of sugar beets, and the money I received financed my first two years in college where I received a teaching certificate. Teaching became my chosen profession. I thought I had it made.

My first employment as a teacher was that of principal of the elementary grades at Ammon, Idaho. Things were going great, and it seemed almost too good to be true in comparison to the difficult time I experienced during my formative years.

Then came the Japanese attack on Pearl Harbor. After finishing the school year, I was drafted into the army and sent to the South Pacific. I was bitter because I had such a good start and felt that if I left, I would never be able to start in such an advantageous position again. I thought about returning to my parents' farm and trying to get an agricultural exemption. Neither of my two older brothers had been called into the service because they were producing food. So if I were included in the farming operation, I might not have to leave and could possibly teach during the off-season.

My mother once again called me in for counseling. After reviewing our history of family hardships, she told me that I was blessed by being born in the covenant in a family of members of the only true church on earth, and that our great nation was the protector of this divine church. She promised me that if I honored the priesthood through my conduct, I would receive countless blessings as promised in my patriarchal blessing. She cautioned that great adversity and hardship would be forthcoming, but if I were faithful to gospel principles I had been taught, including keeping the Word of Wisdom, a way would be opened for me to not only resume a position of gainful employment, but I would be blessed with many new opportunities. I would be made stronger by overcoming the trials and adversities that would come my way.

Because I was leaving for the armed forces shortly, I hurriedly married a young lady I had been dating, feeling that would give me added security upon my return from the service.

I followed my mother's admonitions. I did not knowingly transgress or violate gospel principles. I was the only Mormon in my company, and I did not meet another member of the Church during my entire two years overseas.

In the tropics of the South Pacific, the weather was hot and humid the year round. Having received my temple endowment before entering the service, I wore my garments 24 hours a day as I was instructed to by the temple officiators. I was assigned to a company whose commanding officer was very anti-Mormon. He constantly harassed me about my strange underwear. The weather was so hot and humid that I would soak my blanket with water, spread it out, and lay on top of it to sleep. This officer would come around at night, quietly walk up to where I was sleeping and hit me across the bottom of my feet with a quirt. Then he would laugh loudly and ridicule my garments, making light of the fact that I was wearing them for protection but he was still able to strike me. The torment was difficult to take, but when I corresponded with my parents and related these things to them, they replied: "No matter what hardships you are required to endure, be faithful, and the Lord will bless you for it."

Time went on, and the events of the war became very trying. Many times the doubts coming into my mind were so strong that I felt that everyone, including the Lord, had abandoned me.

In early 1943, my wife gave birth to a baby girl. I was unable to get a leave or furlough to see them. In 1944, I received a letter from her stating that because of my long absence and the loneliness she had suffered, she had met and fallen in love with another man and wanted a divorce.

Shortly after August 15, 1944, I received a cablegram advising me that my brother Lamar, a radioman on a B-17 bomber in the European Theatre of operation, had been shot down and was missing in action. How I anguished and prayed. Because of adversity, I had lost my desire to live. I prayed that if God would preserve the life of my brother, I would gladly surrender mine. Looking back, I knew that some of this was not truly a desire to die but a form of self-pity.

During this period of despair, once again came the message from my parents that the Lord does not break promises. They counseled, "You may not truly comprehend the reason for these hardships and tragedies, but if you will go forward faithfully doing the best you can under the circumstances, you will be blessed."

On September 7, 1944, I had risen early with no particular plans for the day but with a soul full of bitterness and remorse. An explosion occurred. Due to my injuries, a fungus infection in the auditory canals caused scar tissue to form, thus leaving me without ninety percent of my hearing. I saw those about me moving their lips, speaking to me, but heard no sound.

I was left in a world of silence. I was in the deepest of depressions. My health was gone, my marriage deteriorated, a brother was missing in action, and my ability to hear was gone. I believe, from what I can remember, that my prayers were for death. I felt great self-pity. It had been over two years since I had seen someone else who held the priesthood. I had no one to administer to me—no one who was really interested in me since many other soldiers had worse injuries than mine. When a Catholic chaplain associated with the field hospital I was in learned that I could not hear, he just shook his head and went on his way.

Bitterness filled my soul. I began to doubt that the promises made to me by my mother would ever come true. I was over 10,000 miles from home. No one knew of my plight, and I felt no one cared.

I was sent by hospital ship from New Caledonia Field Hospital to San Diego Naval Hospital. When I arrived, no one was there to meet me. I learned later no one had been notified of my situation.

Then a few things started to turn around for the better. The American Red Cross located a telephone with a bone conduction receiver. (The nerves in my ears had not been destroyed so I was able to hear through the specially designed phone.)

The American Red Cross placed a call to my father and mother on October 6, 1944. They were attending LDS General Conference in Salt Lake City, Utah. On the same day, my brother, Lamar, called from New York City. He had walked out of Germany through Luxemburg through enemy lines and was back on friendly turf.

I was forced to stay in the hospital for many months. I first was admitted to Birmingham General Hospital, Van Nuys, California; the Dibble Hospital in

Menlo Park, then Hoff General Hospital in Santa Barbara.

At each place the doctors tried to do something to restore my hearing but to no avail. I was still living in a world of silence and loneliness.

Finally, at Hoff General Hospital I entered a class to learn lip-reading. I was not a very willing patient. I was still suffering from a bad case of self-pity. I knew that I could not return to my teaching position in Ammon, Idaho, because of my hearing deficiency. The therapists told me not to consider any type of public service work or any occupation requiring any verbal or forensic skills. I could possibly be a research worker or an accountant just as long as it did not require sound communciation. I was going nowhere.

Then one day, one grand lady came to see me. Her name was Helen Keller. I could see that she was blind, and I knew from my studies of her life that she was a deaf mute.

I watched her as she was guided among the hosptial beds—astounded at how she communicated in spite of her handicap.

As she came to my bed, someone wrote on a blackboard, "What state is your home state?" Then Captain Harris signaled me to answer. The look on my face must have told him that I knew she could not hear or see me.

He then gently touched Helen Keller as if it were a signal that I did not believe she could communicate with me.

Much to my surprise, she placed her fingers on my lips and her thumb on my trachea and by physical movments urged me to answer the question propounded in writing to me. This I did, and she in turn had another question written for me.

Very sketchily she explained that as long as my health was such that I could not get around that if I would develop the talents I had, the Lord would bless me beyond all measure.

I felt ashamed of the way I had acted and reacted to those who were trying to help me. The words my parents oft repeated to me rang loud and clear in my subconscious, "People are not very impressed with the starts we make; what everybody wants to know is how we finish."

I began enjoying lip reading lessons. It was like playing games. The patients, including myself, would develop a scenario where we would sit on opposite sides of the hospital room and we would have to identify the subject matter that was being discussed without hearing it. Later, we would converse by lip movements with each other until we were able to carry on meaningful conversations.

Finally, the great test came. We were divided into teams of two and handed tickets to Reno, Nevada, for a weekend pass. Without the help of any third party, we were to register in a hotel, order our meals, seek out people to visit, and socialize with them without telling them of our handicap.

The first evening we entered a place of entertainment. Two ladies were sitting in a lounge some 30 to 40 feet from where we were sitting. I was in such a position that I could read their lips. One turned to the other and said, "Do you suppose they are going to pick us up?"

I immediately got to my feet and went over and said, "Sure, where would you like to go?"

The two were flabbergasted. They could not believe they had spoken loudly enough to be heard. They apologized, hurriedly picked up their belongings, and with red faces, left the building without giving us the opportunity to explain what had happened.

My lip reading training continued. I was equipped with a hearing aid weighing approximately five pounds, consisting of a large black box worn under my shirt attached to an ear piece in my right ear and powered by four D batteries which were worn around my belt.

Using a combination of my training in lip reading, aided by some sounds conveyed by the crude hearing aid, I started to mingle with people. I decided that if Helen Keller could mingle and inspire people with her great handicaps, I certainly should be able to function with all the abilities I had left.

I not only disregarded the therapists' admonitions not to go into public service work, I applied to be the manager of the United States Employment Office at Pocatello, Idaho where applicants would come to me for job placements. I was employed as Assistant Manager for one month, then transferred to Idaho Falls as Assistant Manager, and at the end of three months, I was the Manager of the Payette, Idaho, office.

Shortly thereafter, I was offered a position as a rehabilitation officer for the Veterans Administration in Boise, Idaho, to aid and counsel disabled veterans returning home.

This involved interpretations of many public laws. I felt frustrated because I did not feel the interpretations I was getting from my superiors were accurate so I resigned and entered law school at the University of Utah where Spencer L. Kimball was dean of the law school.

He immediately noticed that I was wearing a hearing aid and called me in for counseling, noting that the law course was very demanding even to those who had perfect hearing and wanted to know if he could help me change to a profession where hearing was not such a critical need.

I explained to Brother Kimball that I knew it was not going to be easy, that I had considered the problems my handicap might bring. I told him I could read lips and that if the professors would give me a seat near the front of the room, I would be all right. As for those things the professors said while their backs were turned, I would just have to do that much more reading to make certain I did not miss anything.

I not only finished law school, I finished a four-year course in two and two-thirds years. During my last year in law school, I served as a practitioner in the Salt Lake City Legal Aid Society counseling indigent and handicapped people.

I graduated and returned to Pocatello, Idaho, to set up a practice. I knew not a soul upon whom I could rely to assist me in building my practice.

I read in the paper where one of the senior members of the bar, Judge O. R. Baum, had been hired to handle a major piece of litigation for a large manufacturing company. I meekly applied for a job briefing. I had no references except my law school professors.

At first, Judge Baum turned me down. A short time later, his only son was killed in an auto accident. I received a call late one night asking if I was interested in working for a short time while Judge Baum was recovering from his grief. I gladly accepted. I worked diligently day and night in an effort to show him I could be of worth to him. He seemed mildly pleased with the work, but he associated a more experienced attorney to do the courtroom battles. I resented this kind of treatment then, but now I see it was the right thing to do because of the nature of the complicated considerations involved in courtroom practice.

After some months, it appeared that Judge Baum, who was of advancing age, was about to assume his full practice, and I was given notice to start looking elsewhere for employment.

The Judge was very complimentary and kind, but he did not want to expand his business. I was ready to leave when I received a call advising me that his wife had passed away. He asked me to stay and help him, for he had no family to rely on.

I stayed, and, as a result, I haven't had a day since that I did not have something to do. Because of the people I have met, doors have been opened. I could never have dreamed that I would have the opportunity to serve as an assistant U.S. attorney; city attorney for three cities; general counsel for Shoshone Bannock Tribe; as an expert witness for the U.S. Senate Bureau of Indian Affairs, president of the Idaho Trial Lawyers, etc. Presently I own my own law firm, employing nine people.

While working as a contact rehabilitation officer for the Veterans Administration, I was required to visit local doctors to make sure these doctors would accept veterans as patients if medical or surgical treatment were needed and to see that they received quality treatment at a reasonable cost.

One of these fine surgeons was Dr. O. F. Call in the Kasiska Building in Pocatello. I visited him often because of the fine services he and his nursing staff rendered. I was always greeted by Lucille, a beautiful nurse with naturally curly, jet black hair. Her friendly disposition made me feel welcome, but her stern professional demeanor let me know in no uncertain terms that she had no time for play or gossip. No matter how hard I

tried to get a social dialogue going, she did not let me get
to first base as a Don Juan. She always reminded me
what my job was and that it did not involve entertaining
nurses.

Finally I became desperate. I knew she was the
eternal companion I was dreaming about, but her
interest in me appeared to be no greater than in any
other patient.

I decided to do something to let her know how I
felt. I started sending three roses anonymously every day
to her office hoping to hear some words of recognition
and appreciation. The only thing I heard was how
beautiful those flowers were. I knew in my heart she
knew who was sending them, but she was in full control
with no hint of any credit for my floral offering.

I decided to do something very dramatic. I would
stop her on the office steps, kneel at her feet, tell her how
much I loved her, and propose marriage.

The crucial time came. I rushed up to her, kneeled
at her feet, and started my speech. Lo and behold, the
whole seat of my suit pants split out.

In my embarrassment, I started to take off my suit
coat to cover my posterior. Lucille broke into hilarious
laughter, took the long nursing cape she was wearing,
threw it across both our shoulders to cover my exposed
backside, and said, "Come on, let's go find you another
pair of pants."

The ice was broken, love in all of its splendor
erupted, and the courtship was beautiful. On May 10,
1947, we were married by stake president Alton
Alexander.

Lucille had led a humble life. Born at Pingree,
Idaho, she was one of eight children. Her family were
not members of the LDS Church, but she went with her
friends to Primary, Mutual, and Sunday School. She

learned every principle of righteous living. Her mother died of cancer complicated with pneumonia when Lucille was only 13. She had three younger sisters, the youngest only three years old, so she became the lady of the house. Her father never remarried, and she assisted him in rearing her younger sisters. After Joyce, the youngest, was old enough to fend for herself, Lucille entered nursing school as a full-time, live-in student at St. Anthony Hospital at Pocatello, Idaho.

Under this program she could only go home two weeks a year. She was on call 24 hours a day for three years. During World War II, she joined the Cadet Nurse Corps and graduated in 1945 as a registered nurse. She joined the staff of Dr. O. F. Call and remained there until 1949.

In 1948, when I decided to go to law school, she said, "If you want to go to school, do it. Don't worry. You can go to school in the daytime, and I will work at night. We'll make it."

Our daughter, Cheryl, was born July 8, 1948. We were as poor as church mice and had no way of hiring or paying for a babysitter.

With this great wife's help, I finished my undergraduate work at University of Idaho, Southern Branch and obtained a law degree at the University of Utah.

How well I remember the tremendous sacrifices she made, going without nice clothing, making stew taste like gourmet food, sitting with the baby when measles, mumps, and chicken pox invaded our home—and all this without missing a shift as lead floor nurse at St. Mark's Hospital in Salt Lake City, Utah. I have known Lucille, when illness prevailed in our family, to not lie down and rest for 48 hours straight. I counseled with her, even suggesting that I interrupt my schooling to accept good paying jobs that had been offered me. She always said, "No. Remember, it's not how you start, it's how you finish that people really care about."

She has been my wife, my lover, my counselor, and my strength. Not only did she care for me but for our three children (Cheryl, Charlene, and Monte. Charlene was born June 11, 1953, and Monte June 28, 1955). I cannot thank her enough. We are grateful for all our blessings and for being sealed February 25, 1977, in the Idaho Falls Temple. We appreciate our strong testimonies of the gospel of Jesus Christ and the joy living the principles brings into our lives.

I testify that the Lord does not break promises. If we diligently try to perform our responsibilities and duties even in the face of trials and adversity, great will be our reward and we will be made stronger. I know that if we are faithful to our covenants and callings, we not only benefit ourselves but we benefit those around us by our example.

My opportunity to see and be with Helen Keller was momentary when considering the overall span of time, but she, by her example and spirit, gave my life purpose and a sense of direction that was missing until then, and by this inspirational soul taking time out of her life to touch my lips and let me know there was a way—it is my firm belief a soul was saved.

R. Max Whittier
March, 1984

THE LORD'S HAND
SAVED BENJI'S LIFE

The Fourth of July weekend, 1976, holds many memories for all of us. As a nation we celebrated the two hundredth anniversary of our country, but for me, my three-year-old son, Benjamin, and all of us attending the Hopkin family reunion at Star Valley, Wyoming, that weekend holds even more meaning.

The reunion was held in the woods, with each family in campers or tents around the campground. After we arrived about noon, I was on the way to the car, about 200 feet distant, to get some baby food for our ten-month-old, Nathan. On the path I met Benjie, who proudly announced that he and his newfound buddies (older cousins) were going on a hike. I remember smiling to myself as I watched him march behind the others. His overalls were too short, and his red socks bounced up and down with each step.

I went on to the car and obtained the food. On my way back, I travelled on the path in the opposite direction I had seen Benjie and the others go not five minutes before. As I walked, I could hear the baby's cries coming through the woods. I didn't want him to bother the others, so I decided to take the food to him and come back later to check on Benjie.

I turned my body towards the camp, but my feet kept going straight, causing me to stumble and nearly fall. I walked faster and faster, as if going down hill or as if a force were behind my feet, pushing them every step. I still didn't know why I was doing it.

I came to a stream and saw a pair of little shoes on the bank with a pair of bright red socks neatly laid across them. I called, "Benjie," and looked down into the stream. Some of the other youngsters had blocked off the stream to make a swimming hole. I saw only a limp arm and Benjie's little blue face turned towards me. I'll never forget the look on his face. His mouth was open as if he were trying to call me. I don't remember going in after him, but I remember putting him over my shoulder, expelling water from his airway passage. He began to sputter and gasp for breath. Later he vomited a great amount of water. I knew his little body had taken in all the water it could hold.

After we were sure Benjie was going to be all right, the family knelt in prayer to thank our Heavenly Father for his great blessing of preserving Benjie's life. Our hearts were full of gratitude and joy.

After coming so close to death, Benjie had trouble sleeping and often awoke with nightmares. We decided not to talk to him about his experience until he was older and able to talk about the fear and anxiety he had experienced.

A few weeks later, Benjie was playing while I was vacuuming. I saw him jump off a chair and thrash about on the floor; and I witnessed that look on his face, the same he had when he was in the water. I turned off the vacuum and asked him to tell me about what he was doing. He said, "When we were in Wyoming I decided to go swimming by myself, so I took my shoes off and jumped in, but I couldn't stand up. I tried to call you, Mama, but the water got in my throat, so Heavenly

Father went to you and brought you where I was so you could get me out."

That was exactly the feeling I had experienced. It wasn't just a prompting. Someone actually came and took me to my son. I will never forget that feeling, and I will never cease to be grateful to our kind and loving Heavenly Father for his protecting hand.

I have a testimony of the Lord's influence in our lives and that he lives and answers prayers. May we always show our gratitude and faith in him by the way we exemplify his teachings.

LeAnn Barrus Mitchell
June, 1981

FAITH IN PRAYER

It was the summer of 1983, and my family was preparing for our six-hour trip to Santaquin, Utah, for our vacation with our grandparents.

Mom was inside the house putting together the final necessities we would need for the trip. Dad hadn't come home from work, and since we were waiting for him, we probably wouldn't leave for another hour or two. In the meantime, Mom asked me to go buy some pop for the trip. She said, "Take the pickup and first go see your dad at work at the Targhee National Forest Service Building in St. Anthony and get some money from him."

Being a care-free fifteen-year-old teen-ager, I jumped at the chance to drive Dad's most important worldly possession. Inside his office, I explained to him about Mom's request. He took out his wallet and handed me a fifty-dollar bill. I still remember his specific words of warning. "Here's a fifty. Now be careful. Buy the pop and give the change to Mom as we'll need it for gas to go to Utah. Tell her I'll be home in a couple of hours." With a quick "Thank-you. I love you, Dad," I was off to the store.

After making my purchase, hastily I took the change and got back in the pickup. Instead of putting the change carefully in my pocket, I threw the loose coins in the back with the pop and dropped the two twenty-dollar bills in my lap.

Upon returning home, I ran to the house with the sack. Thinking only about going to Utah, I completely forgot about the change. I started carrying out suitcases and helping Mom pack. After I'd taken out the last suitcase, she asked the question I soon came to regret. "Where is the change?"

I had forgotten to grab it when I jumped out of the pickup. The bills had fallen on the ground although they weren't there when I went back for them. Together Mom and I searched. Since the wind had been blowing, I figured they could be anywhere. We have a couple of granaries, a couple of horsesheds, some corrals, and a barn next to our dirt driveway.

Within ten minutes Mom found one bill in the corral. I breathed a sigh of relief and continued to search for the other bill. We looked everywhere, under rocks, behind boards, and between various things. It was absolutely nowhere to be found.

As we were close to giving up, we were both inspired to look in the haystack. We searched it from top to bottom, knowing it could be lodged in any little crack since I had wadded both bills in my hand. It was to no avail.

I then went into the barn, got down on my knees, and prayed to my Father in Heaven. I first thanked him for his many blessings to me and for my opportunity to live upon this beautiful earth, to be a member of The Church of Jesus Christ of Latter-day Saints, and to know its teachings are true. Then I asked him if it didn't seem too selfish for me to ask, to please help us find the other twenty-dollar bill. I closed "In the name of Jesus Christ, Amen," and left the barn.

Again Mom and I were inspired to look in the haystack. We lifted the first bale of hay off the stack, and there it was. It was flat and crisp and appeared to be a brand new bill. It was unbelievable how an old, crumpled-up twenty could appear new and flat and, of all places, under a bale of hay. Then I realized how it could have happened. Tears welled up in our eyes. When I told Mom about praying and how my prayer had been answered, she told me that she, too, had prayed for Heavenly Father's direction. I certainly gained a testimony that he hears and answers our prayers, and at that moment, I felt very close to him. I humbly thank him for wanting to know our needs and to realize that he listens to our prayers.

Angie Johnson, 18
June, 1986

THAT'S MY MAMA

I had a special, faith-promoting experience in Ogden, Utah, in 1971 when my daughter, Angie who is now 18, was about 3 years old. She and I were grocery shopping in a huge warehouse store where people bagged their own groceries and used a flat cart instead of a basket cart with a child's seat in it.

Angie grew tired quickly as small children do and wanted to go. I tried to assure her we would leave soon, that I only had one more aisle to check for needed supplies. I was busy looking and selecting items. The moment I reached the end of the aisle, I realized I had lost her.

I didn't panic at first. I immediately left my groceries and checked up and down each aisle. I asked a few people if they had seen a little blue-eyed, blonde girl in red shorts. No one seemed to have seen her or even acted as if they cared. Then I did panic. I asked myself all the questions mothers would under such circumstances. "Why hadn't I left when she said she was tired? Why hadn't I picked her up and carried her? Where could she be?" I didn't know where to look or what to do.

I said a silent prayer and asked Heavenly Father for help. The next thing I knew I was walking through the store door, across the parking lot past my car, across a four-lane highway into the K-Mart parking lot, and to the K-Mart front doors. All the time I kept asking myself, "What are you doing? Where are you going? No three-year-old would come all the way over here. There's no possible way she could have crossed the highway."

While frantically considering these things, I walked to the K-Mart customer service desk. I was just starting to tell my story when I heard Angie say, "That's my mama."

I looked up, and there she was holding a lady's hand. Angie was calm and not the least bit frightened.

Any mother would know how I reacted. My mind was full of questions. "How and why had she left? How did she ever make it that far?" All I could do was hold her tightly in my arms and cry, thanking Heavenly Father over and over again for answering my prayer.

As we walked out of the store, across the parking lot, across the four lanes of traffic and through the grocery store parking lot, I again could not comprehend how she had made it all the way by herself. I asked, "Angie, how did you get across the big road?" She said, "A man took me." I couldn't believe someone would take a child across a highway and leave her alone. So I asked, "Angie, what did this man look like?" She looked up at me and said solemnly, "He looked like Jesus, Mommy." I picked her up in my arms again and hugged her all the way home.

When we arrived home with no groceries, my husband, Tim, wondered what had occurred. I had forgotten to return to the store for them.

I have not told this special story to many people, but it will always be in my heart and a part of my fervent testimony that our Heavenly Father does listen to and answer our prayers.

Peggie Greenhalgh Johnson

PRAYER—FAITH, KEY AND DOOR
TO HEAVEN

My wife, the former Helen Aileen Nielsen, and I were anticipating the arrival of a new baby, hopefully Christmas Day, 1943.

I was working in Richmond, Utah, seven miles south of where we resided at Franklin, Idaho, when a friend and a relative came to me one day. They excitedly announced, "Your wife says to come immediately."

Dr. Cragan, of Lewiston, Utah, had been notified of Aileen's threatening needs. He and I arrived about the same time in response to her plea. We had explicit faith in Dr. Cragan for he was well known and respected throughout the valley, especially for his success with maternity cases. However, I felt great apprehension as four years earlier Aileen had lost a stillborn baby daughter because she hadn't dilated sufficiently. After examiing her, he assured me, "This will be a natural birth."

"Bring me two containers, one with ice cold water and one with water so hot that you can't stand a finger in it." A tiny baby girl soon arrived, blue and seemingly lifeless. He immersed her alternately in cold, then hot water several times and finally our baby Alice gasped and cried out. Dr. Cragan handed her to Julia Hobbs, a dear neighbor and friend, who gave her the usual rub-down.

Aileen had a moment to adore Alice before Julia prepared her for her crib.

We wondered if Alice should be rushed to the hospital at Salt Lake City or to the one in Ogden, Utah. In his usual, kindly manner, Dr. Cragan replied, "Floyd, if you save this baby, you and your wife must do it yourselves. Neither hospital is equipped adequately for preemies, and she may not receive the care she needs." Since no scales were available, Dr. Cragan guessed Alice weighed 3 pounds and 3/4 ounces and was approximately 19 inches tall. Our Christmas baby had arrived three months early on September 24th!

Alice's bed was a wicker basket with a wicker bottom placed on a vanity seat with blankets inside and outside of the basket to the floor. We kept the vanity seat over the furnace heat vent. Inside the basket we placed water bags and fruit jars filled with warm water. We moved our bed close by so we could frequently touch our darling. If she seemed the least bit clammy, we took her to the warmed oven of the electric stove. This system went on night after night.

Attempting to feed Alice was a frustrating experience. For some time, it took over an hour to get her to take an ounce of milk. On two different occasions, we called our doctor to come as quickly as possible to awaken her as we had had no success.

Aileen tenderly cared for Alice during the day, and I relieved her nights. We were becoming exhausted as well as fearful for our baby's life. We pondered what action to take. There was a small barn at the bottom of our lot. One day soon after these helpless feelings had overwhelmed us, I went to a secluded spot near the barn. With faith in our Heavenly Father, I knelt down and again poured my heart out to him, pleading that he would preserve our baby's life. After a half an hour, these welcome words came to me, "You shall rear your child to maturity."

Upon returning to the house, I related to my wife what had happened and told her to cease worrying, that all would be well. Thereafter, everything was much easier and we felt richly blessed. Our little one grew and developed. It took her one year, though, to double her weight.

Later we became alarmed over Alice's growth pattern. Five different doctors examined her and said she was perfectly normal. When she was nineteen, Dr. Tyler of the University Medical Center at Salt Lake City was recommended to us. After giving her an extensive examination, he exclaimed, "I'm sorry. There's nothing that can be done about your daughter's growth. Her bone ends have already hardened." What a shock this was to us and to Alice. We had kept her back one year from starting first grade. When she did attend school, she tired easily and returned home exhausted from doing school work and walking the three blocks. She often went directly to her room and slept two hours.

When Alice was in high school, but mostly after high school, she became proficient in sewing skills, having learned from her mother. She made her own attractive, well-fitted clothes. How proud we were of her efforts.

In July, 1967, Alice sustained a sudden heartbreak. Her mother, with whom she had been very close, was diagnosed as having a malignant brain tumor. She passed away the following month, the year before Alice's graduation from South Cache High School at Hyrum, Utah. Alice willingly assumed a lot of the responsibility of caring for our home after Aileen's death, as well as helping in our greenhouse and floral business in Hyrum.

Alice attended Utah State University at Logan on state rehabiliitation funds, taking interior and fabric design. She also learned to weave beautifully on her loom. She worked for her advisor, Jessie Larsen, in the Art Department during her last year at USU, and after graduation worked as a teacher's aide. In 1972, she certified in elementary education. Unable to obtain a position in Cache Valley or Logan, Utah, she moved to Ammon, near Idaho Falls, in 1977, and was soon hired to teach kindergarten in Bonneville School District #93. She loved the little boys and girls and is now enjoying teaching first grade.

One memorable highlight of our lives was for Alice and me to tour Europe in September, 1974. She made all the necessary preparations and took care of the daily schedules.

I thank my Heavenly Father for saving this lovely young lady's life, for the joy and happiness she brings to me, and for her many achievements. If she has shed tears over the "slights" and "static" she has encountered, as she refers to her trials, they have been shed when she was alone. I know God hears and answers our prayers and that faith unlocks the door. I know the restored gospel of Jesus Christ is the true plan of life and exaltation. Our happiness here and hereafter is determined by our adherence to it.

Floyd H. Bradford
March, 1987

GOD ANSWERS PRAYERS

It was a typical Saturday morning: linens to change, lawns to mow, floors crying to be done, and Saturday morning cartoons needing to be turned down.

I was just contemplating how delightful the shade of the park would feel if we all pitched in and were done with our work by noon. Typically, however, just as I began the plans in my mind, the phone rang. It was John Bills (the world's most caring and dedicated social worker) asking, "How are you doing?" And, of course, I knew that was merely the prelude.

"Fine," I answered, my mind memorizing the inflections in his voice, trying to pre-guess the rest of his call, in particular, how many children his call would mean.

"Are you ready for two more?" he asked.

I looked around: Cheerios floated in milk puddles beneath the high chair; the dryer bell sounded, announcing, "Another load to fold." Popeye was rescuing Olive Oil just as our daughter, Bree, tripped on the TV cord, and a spontaneous chorus arose from the other children breathlessly awaiting the outcome.

"Sure, John," I heard myself say. (Who could say "No" to John, knowing of the hundreds of hours and prayers he spends on behalf of kids?)

After a telephone conversation with my husband, Rex, a glance at the clock told me we had an hour and forty-five minutes before our new foster children would arrive. We quickly sorted out the mechanics and sprang into action. Another crib needed to be set up, and the trundle bed needed a pillow.

Each little one who comes to our door is a special child, precious to our Father in Heaven. Our task is to help each one feel loved, secure, and at peace for whatever length of time he is part of our family.

How my heart ached as I looked at a two-year-old with scars from belt-buckle beatings on his head and the rest of his body. And although I couldn't see the scars and bruises on the inside, I knew they were there, multiplied.

I'll never forget the seven-year-old boy who held tightly to John's hand and sobbed when he left. John was the only friend he had known during his short and painful life. The baby who came after spending several weeks in the intensive care unit at the hospital will always hold a special place in our hearts. He had been so badly mistreated that he was afraid to cry aloud. It was three months and thousands of hugs and kisses later that we heard his first cry. We'll always remember that day. With grateful tears we rushed in to meet his needs.

One day, three little girls came to spend a few weeks with us. They had such a horrible odor it was difficult to get close to them. They walked in like toy soldiers, no expression in their eyes, no meaning in their walk, and no hope or trust in their faces. What a thrill was ours when we first heard their giggles, watched them run and play, felt and observed the living, vivacious peace in their faces. All in all, we have had over twenty different little ones in and out of our home within a few years.

When Marc came, we all stood and stared at him. Even the dog stood still as we looked at tear-stained cheeks, tattered clothes, and brown, bare feet. We had never seen such a sad and lonely child or felt such despair and torment.

I reached out my hand, wanting to hold him in my arms and hug away his tears, but he instinctively withdrew. Rex tried to talk to him, but his whole being remained the same. It was only after the children tried to talk to him and took turns at "show and tell," that he began to relax. Oh, how we prayed, "Dear Father, please help us get through to Marc. Please show us the way to break through his shell so he can learn to feel, trust, and love."

One Friday, the way was opened. We heard our son, Steve, yell, "Help." Everyone ran to see what tragedy had happened. (We found later that it wasn't a tragedy, but the answer to our prayers.) All six rabbits had escaped from their pen, and every available person was desperately needed.

"Marc, grab that one!" shouted our daughter, Shari, and the chase was on. Mom, Dad, kids, dogs, and rabbits were running in all directions. All the confusion that could possibly accompany a rabbit chase was there in our backyard.

Marc grabbed the one he had chased into a corner and squealed with delight as he felt the rabbit's soft fur. His eyes wide in wonderment, he gathered it close to hold, hug, and gently rock. Marc became a real part of our family that day. Later, after all the rabbits were captured, dogs were quieted, and the family completely exhausted sitting on the lawn, we saw a triumphant grin on Marc's face. His eyes sparkled, and we knew he felt the joy of having done his part well. We know that God answers prayers. Today Marc isn't with us physically, but he'll always be in our hearts and prayers.

To the question, "Are *all* these kids yours?" the answer is a simple "Yes," because from the moment they come to the door until they leave, they are a part of our family. Many times we hear the question, "Why do you do it?" or "How do you do it?" I have always felt that homes should be open to all in need, so a better question would be, "Why not do it?" and to that I have no answer.

I can only say that we are a family most blessed. We have assuredly grown from our experience. Each little one has shown us a new dimension of life. We have truly learned a lot about love, patience, and sharing. It hasn't all been pleasant, but we have no regrets unless that we might and should have done more.

We are humbly grateful for our "forever children": Steve, 11; Shari, 10; Bree Anne, 8; Brandon, 6; Cami, 5; and Chandi, 3; for their part in our efforts to help others. They traded beds and shared their rooms, toys, and treasures. For the most part, the challenge has been theirs to make a lonely, frightened child feel like part of the family. Hand in hand with Rex, we really do believe the saying, "A home filled with love has elastic arms."

The lesson of "loving thy neighbor as thyself" was taught by example in my parents' home as long as I can remember. Compassion for others was just a way of life. My father and mother, Max W. and Evelyn Craner, were always doing something for somebody.

My grandparents also helped instill in me that each and every child of God has a certain task to accomplish in this life. Part of our task has been to lighten the lives of others and hopefully lighten their burdens.

We are humbly grateful for our membership in The Church of Jesus Christ of Latter-day Saints. It is a constant reminder to me of the teachings I received at home as a child, and it gives Rex and me a guide by which to rear our children.

I know that God lives and that he cares about and loves each of us *individually*. That is what is so exciting.

I just pray that Rex and I, with the help of our Heavenly Father who loves us most, can give some of that excitement to our children and to every child with whom we come in contact, making them aware that they, and we, are children of our Heavenly Father.

It was a typical Saturday morning when John Bills called as the prelude to our day . . . and now our challenge is to ease from the prelude into the song; and with time, prayer, and love, develop comfortable harmony.

Diane Craner Brown
February, 1984

A FLIGHT TO REMEMBER

As I checked the weather from my bedroom window that morning in June, 1975, my heart was full. I silently thanked God for our many blessings.

My husband, Jinks, had passed away not quite a year previously, and the past three years had been difficult for our family. But this particular morning my heart was filled with gratitude and hope. Our son, Lee, had been called to serve in the Argentina Cordoba Mission and was to enter the mission home in Salt Lake City, Utah on June 14. His testimonial had already been held in the St. Anthony Third Ward.

Today he was to take his prized possession—his car—to a friend in Aberdeen, Idaho. Another friend, Terry Wade of Shelley, who had recently been called to serve a mission in Switzerland, was going with him; I was to pick them up later that morning and bring them home.

The sky was clear; the sun was rising, filling our valley with that beautiful glow which is such a blessed part of Idaho mornings—a pilot's dream. As we prepared for the day, everything seemed so right.

My plane was a Piper Tripacer. It represented three years of "tender loving care." I had rebuilt it under Jinks' direction. Birthdays and special days were a part of this little gem; the radio, compass, tachometer, and many other parts were gifts from my loving family. It was my pride and joy. So as I opened the hangar doors and pulled the plane out, for the first time in ever so long, my thoughts were carefree and happy.

The flight to Aberdeen was very relaxing, and the boys were waiting on schedule.

I knew my left tank wasn't full, but since I had a full right tank, I felt there was no fuel problem. My switch was not letter perfect, however, so I decided to change tanks while on the ground. As I turned the switch, I felt the click indicating the lever to the right tank had caught. All was still OK.

After some small talk with Terry and Lee and a bit of looking about the Aberdeen airport, we loaded up. We charted our course straight to the Idaho Falls airport and headed home. Lee and Terry talked, and I listened, happy in the knowledge I was privileged to be with such choice spirits and feel their eagerness about their missions. It was a wonderful experience for me to have.

After we passed Blackfoot, I noted we were well ahead of schedule. The area between Aberdeen and Idaho Falls is mostly lava flow. A straight course takes in more lava than going around but saves time and is often used. Blackfoot was to my right and just behind as I entered the Rose area located northeast of Blackfoot.

Suddenly all was quiet. Quiet is a good word and welcome, but not at 6,000 feet. At once I realized the switch had not worked; I was not using gas from the right tank but from the left, and I was out of gas.

Now the Tripacer is not a big plane, and at 6,000 feet I had very little space to play with. I looked the area over; so did Lee and Terry. We were just breaking over the lava and could see a road below us, a man on a tractor, and a bridge with power lines. On one side was farm ground with a sprinkler pipe running through, on the other a triangular shaped area with lava jutting out. This seemed the best place to land.

Many things passed through my mind in those few moments. But there was no panic. As I recall, the only remark made was that the boys now knew that the main purpose of a prop was to keep the pilot cool. "Protect your faces," I warned. And down we went.

As we neared the ground—and this came mighty fast—I touched the rudder, heading us a bit to the right. Then, in an effort to miss the piece of lava jutting out on the right side, I endeavored to slip the plane to the left a little with the rudder. This automatically lowered the left wing since a Tripacer has interlocking aileron and rudder controls. My next recollection was seeing two boys with lots of blood on them. What a relief it was to hear them exclaim, "We're all right." Upon impact, I had been sitting forward and had hit the instrument panel. The boys had gotten out of the plane and carried me out, fearing fire. However, the right wing had not been hit. Our worst problem was a badly damaged plane.

Directly over where Lee's head should have been was a piece of tubing (a brace for the cockpit). This was bent down so that had he been there it would have crushed his head. However, he was leaning over trying to protect me and was not touched. Terry was also not seriously injured.

I was first taken to a Blackfoot hospital and then to the Pocatello airport by ambulance. From there I was flown to the LDS Hospital at Salt Lake City, where I remained about four days. My injuries were quite extensive: a broken sternum, left hand and wrist, and nose. Numerous facial lacerations caused me to lose a lot of blood. After I had plastic surgery and was able to leave the hospital, my brother Hollis Cordingley, and his wife, Donna, took care of me in their home. They also attended to the needs of our family, for which love and concern I shall always be grateful.

Although this accident caused much anxiety and work for my four daughters, I never heard a complaint from one of them as they helped their brother with his final mission preparations.

It would have been very disappointing not to go with Lee to the mission home, but Hollis and Donna felt I was well enough to go with them to take Lee.

Later when one of the FAA inspectors flew with me over the accident area while giving me a check ride, which is customary any time there is an accident, he told me he thought my choice for a landing spot was the best one and that the incident had been handled correctly.

At this time, October, 1987, Lee and Terry are both happily married and diligent in their Church service; Georgiann, Deon, and Leandra are likewise happily married and have lovely families. My youngest daughter, Penny, is making us all proud as she serves in the South Carolina Columbia Mission.

As a result of this experience, our whole family realized many things: the importance of missionary work, that through faith and prayer we *can* and *do receive* needed help from our Heavenly Father, and how fragile and unimportant material things are. And my testimony was indeed strengthened. I know God heard our prayers on that precarious flight—one which we'll always remember—and that Lee and Terry needed to fill their missions.

I also know that I did not land that plane by myself. During the entire time we had a feeling, which is hard for me to explain, but which I recognize could have only come from one source. I know that through faith, fasting, and prayer, we can receive help with any problem we have. Memories of this incident make me keenly aware that material things are only of this world and should be viewed in that perspective. The only important things are what we can take with us: our knowledge of and love we show our Heavenly Father and his son, Jesus Christ, and our love and service to others.

Margaret C. Stanford

REWARDS THROUGH SERVICE

Our family's experience with the LDS Church's Indian Placement Program goes back to 1967. Ralph and Carol Cutler of the Seattle Eighth Ward had an Indian boy come to live with them. To my knowledge, that was the first year of the program in Washington. My husband, Monte, was in his last year of orthodontic school at the University of Washington, and he informed me of his desire to participate in this program the following year.

The fall of 1968 found us and our children, Marianne, Kristi, Robert, and Richard awaiting the arrival of our first Lamanite student, Patricia Birdsbill. We drove to the Seattle stake center to meet her. She looked beautiful but seemed very shy. While we were waiting for the processing to be completed, a feeling of nausea came over me and Monte had to bring the car to the nearest door. As I lay on the carseat, I wondered what this young girl thought of her new foster mother. Here I was with a cast on my leg (a result of a fall down some stairs) and feeling sick. Upon our arrival home, Monte helped me to go inside, and then, of all things, I had a miscarriage. Despite the unusual beginning, we had a happy home life with Patricia and were excited to have her.

She was a lovely, creative girl who did well in art classes and was on the school gymnastic team. She loved dancing lessons at Verla Flowers Dance Arts. She and our daughters became very close. At the end of the school year, Patricia returned home to Wolf Point, Montana.

That summer we decided to give Pat's parents an opportunity to meet her foster family, and we certainly wanted to meet them so we could be a better foster family by knowing and understanding them. While at Wolf Point, we presented the idea of their being sealed in the temple when they came to Pat's graduation in a couple of years.

Brother Birdsbill (Charlie) indicated that he and his wife, Loverty, had not thought that would be possible and, naturally, they were both thrilled with the prospect.

Kathy, another Birdsbill daughter, had been on the program in a different area and did not plan to return. We asked her if she would consider coming to Seattle with Pat and living with us, too. She consented to this arrangement. I think Monte was the only foster father with four daughters at the Ingraham High Father-Daughter Banquet the next year.

Brother William Bush, coordinator of the Indian Placement Program at the time (presently a mission president), was a good influence for us. He told us there would be good days and bad days and that we might eventually feel or might never feel that our time with these young people was successful. He stressed that this should not be our reason for participating in the program. He said we should love them and help them better their lives.

We had many hours of worry and concern as Pat returned each year from the reservation, her love renewed for an Indian lad whose ideals were very different from her own. Pat's mind was closed many times to the numerous blessings and opportunities within her grasp as she tried to hold onto her youthful love.

Her family came from Wolf Point in June 1971 for the joyous occasion to see their fifth child be their first graduate from high school.

While staying with us, Brother Birdsbill, who had converted from Catholicism to Mormonism a few years before, had many discussions with and bore his testimony to Jim Lau, a young Catholic friend of ours. Jim was visiting us from Hawaii, and Brother Birdsbill undoubtedly helped him realize the truthfulness of the teachings of the LDS Church, for Jim later joined.

The Don Anderton family also had a Birdsbill daughter, Annie, on the Placement Program. They joined our family in taking Brother and Sister Birdsbill, eight of their children, and one granddaughter to Salt Lake City where Pat, Marianne, and Kristi performed in the All-Church Dance Festival and Kathy sang in the regional Youth Choir at general conference. At this time the Anderton's son, Mike, entered the mission home prior to leaving for Chile. At the temple, he witnessed the sealing of eight of the twelve Birdsbill children and one deceased child to their parents. This experience, along with attendance at BYU in the fall, brought a great spiritual change in Pat. She had many wonderful experiences while performing with the Lamanite Generation. It was here she and another performer, Harry "Courage" Benally, met. They were married in the fall of 1972 in the Ogden Temple ten days after the birth of our fifth child, Thomas. After her marriage, we returned to Seattle and gave a reception for Pat and Courage so their many friends could extend their love and best wishes to them.

After Courage and Pat had five lovely children (one deceased), their marriage ended in divorce. Pat is now married to Mazo McCabe, a civil engineer, and they live in Billings, Montana. They have added a son to their sweet family.

Kathy graduated from Ingraham High School in 1972 and is now living in Wolf Point.

The Birdsbill's son, Alan, lived with us for three years while attending school. Much to our disappointment, Alan chose to return home when his Wolf Point friends left the program. Brother Birdsbill served as a member of the branch presidency for a period of time, and Loverty was in the Relief Society presidency. Because of their love for the Church, five of their daughters and one son participated in the Placement Program. Two younger sons remained in Wolf Point.

An added blessing which came about because of our participation in the program is that when Mike Anderton returned from his mission in the summer of 1973, he married his foster sister's foster sister, our daughter, Kristi, in the Ogden Temple. Previous to this event, our oldest daughter, Marrianne, married Scott Nash in the Logan Temple after his mission to France. Rob and Rick also served missions: Rob in the Spain Barcelona Mission, and Rick in the Colombia Bogata Mission. If these details do not seem relevant to this experience, they will be of interest to the Birdsbill family and to our own, as through the years, we have become very close.

As we look back, some things that stand out in our minds as the greatest rewards through our service in the Indian Placement Program are: the sealing of the Birdsbill family, Jim Lau's conversion, and Mike Anderton's marriage to our Kristi. Who knows what other far-reaching effects our experience may have?

Monte and I enjoy and appreciate our callings in the Church and our civic responsibilities. Sometimes we feel we're almost too involved. But life is not meant to be easy. When we are told that we are to "work out our salvation," I believe *work* is the key. If we voluntarily take part in all the Church has to offer, the Lord is most generous in bestowing his blessings upon us. I am humbly grateful for the knowledge that Jesus is the Christ and that if we can follow his example, we will once again live with him and our Father in Heaven. That all of our family may do this and help others to do the same is forever our goal.

Eunice Tidwell Merrill
April, 1985

MIKE'S ACCIDENT INFLUENCES OUR FAITH AND WORKS

It started out to be such a typical Saturday that February 16, 1980, with shopping, piano lessons, and the usual errands to do, but late in the afternoon when I turned the corner down my street, I saw a fire truck and aide car two houses beyond mine.

As I got out of the car, my neighbors came running. By the expressions on their faces, I knew it involved a member of my family.

Michael, five-and-one-half years old, had been playing with his friends. Due to the unusual amount of snow we had had a month earlier, a deep pond had formed due to the runoff from the lake near us. The boys had been playing near the edge when our neighbor's dog, Bambi, fell through the thin ice. Mike and Matthew Kitchener, age seven, both tried to help the dog and each other, but the water was so cold and deep that they both fell in. The two Hamlin boys (Jason and Jared) ran to get their dad, Randy, and my husband, Brad. When Brad arrived, he saw Mike's bright red-orange coat on top of the water and pulled him out.

Someone commenced CPR, but there was no heartbeat. My husband and Randy searched for Matt, but couldn't locate him. By that time, the firemen were pulling Brad out of the icy water. They immediately treated him for hyperthermia. The next few hours became a blur, and the days seemed to run together. Our hearts ached for Alice Kitchener as her son, Matthew, was found by someone at the bottom of the pond, but he couldn't be saved, even by doctors. This accident was doubly hard on her as her husband had died about two months previously. On the morning of that fateful day, Matt was overheard to say, "I wish I could see my dad just one more time." I'm sure his dad was there!

Many prayers were offered and blessings given as we waited to see if our Michael would live. The doctors didn't offer much hope because he had been under water nearly a half hour, and they tried to prepare us for the amount of possible brain damage.

When I look back now, I wonder how we survived that horrible nightmare. Our faith was truly tested and is still being tested. Our Heavenly father helped us through those two and one-half months Mike was in the hospital and also as we prepared to bring him home. Even after I received special training, I can honestly say my confidence was near zero.

Michael was exteremely weak, and our main concern was that his swallowing ability was also very weak and choking was a constant possibility. He required feeding through a tube inserted surgically into his stomach.

What are some of the blessings we have received from this experince? *For one thing, we have really learned to rely on the Lord.* So often when Mike was in some kind of difficulty after we had done everything we could for him, Brad simply laid his hands on Mike's head and gave him a father's blessing. Always Mike calmed down and went to sleep before his dad finished the blessing. Brad's faith and spirituality have increased ten-fold as he has watched his prayers being answered time and time again.

We have learned compassion. Not only have we become more loving and giving with each other, but I have been amazed at the love and concern other people showed for us. Members of the church that we didn't even know took turns going to the Children's Orthopedic Hospital to be with our little boy so he wouldn't be lonely. In fact, so many people visited him that whenever the nurses saw anyone standing around in the halls or looking lost, they automatically directed them to Mike's room! The nurses and doctors were very impressed with the support and concern of Church members. Even our three-year-old, Trevor, has learned compassion. One day he fell and hurt himself, and as I was giving him a love and saying what a big boy he was, he smiled through his tears and said, I'm going to grow really big and strong, Mama, so I can carry Michael."

We've learned to sacrifice as we've all been involved in Mike's care. Travis and Trevor help me bathe him, and our daughters, Robin and Pam, know how to feed, suction, and turn him. He doesn't move much on his own, so he has to be turned from side to side often to prevent bed sores. Todd, our ten-year-old, is learning to do these things. Our children have also had to learn how to deal with Mike's vomiting and seizures since both are frequent and frightening.

We've learned endurance and patience. Many times I've felt that I just couldn't bear to put one foot in front of the other one more time. After I prayed, it was as though the Lord had taken my hand and was helping me to continue on.

One of the biggest problems I've encountered, especially during the first few months, was memories of Michael before his accident. So many tears have been shed and on many days I prayed constantly for those memories to be taken away until I could learn to handle them. Presently, it is mid-November, 1981, and I know each day we've been given strength and renewed faith and can expect similar blessings in the future.

Brad and I are grateful for the gospel of Jesus Christ, for the knowledge of life after death, for the fact that we know what the future has in store for Michael, and not just for this life either. We are grateful to know that he is a celestial child and is going through this trial to help his family obtain the celestial kingdom.

We are very grateful to the doctors and nurses who took such excellent care of him and to the many people who supported us with their prayers; for the women who took care of our little ones so I could be at the hospital, and especially the women who came in twice daily for a period of time to help with Mike's therapy. I'm grateful to my Relief Society visiting teachers for their love, help, and strength.

The support of our family and friends mean a lot to us. Within a few hours after the accident, many waited at the hospital with us, and the next day, my mom, Stella Roberts, and my sister, Joyce Hathaway, flew in from St. Anthony, Idaho, and Brad's brother Randy from Salt Lake City to lend their support. Brad's parents, Verla and Elmer Roberts, have also been outstanding examples of humility and steadfastness during this crucial experience.

We know there will still be many trials, but knowing that our Heavenly Father loves us and continually strengthens us to get through this trial, we can trust him to help us with anything else he deems necessary for our salvation.

Whenever I'm worried or upset about Michael's condition and I voice my concerns to the Lord, I receive such a peaceful, contented awareness and an almost excited feeling comes over me and the words flash through my mind that I am not to worry about Mike, but to just have patience and faith and everything will work out for the best where he is concerned.

May this experience and testimony help others who may be experiencing difficult tests. I do know that there isn't one person who will ever live on this earth who won't be tried and tested, and that each of us will be judged on the way we handle and accept adversity. We feel at times that we have been plunged to the depths of despair, but the one thing we cling to is our faith in our Heavenly Father. We know he loves our family and he won't require us to go through any more than we can handle. He will always provide a way.

Stella R. Roberts
November, 1981

FROM THE SPIRIT WORLD

I am thankful I was born of goodly parents, John and Eliza Sorensen Roberts. It gives me a thrill to read their histories and reflect on their lives. They endured the hardships of pioneer life. My father joined the Church in Wales, and my mother, in Denmark. They came with their families to Utah before the advent of the railroad. Father walked across the plains. The older I get, the more I appreciate their teachings and the things they did for me. They taught me the gospel by example as well as by precept.

I appreciated having the priesthood in my home when I was growing up. Since my marriage, I have enjoyed the blessings of the priesthood my husband, William J. Lewis, has held. I know that the calls which have come to us through the priesthood have brought us many blessings and untold joy.

It has been our privilege to have many of the General Authorities visit our home during the years 1945-1957 when my husband served as president of the Yellowstone Stake. I have deeply appreciated their wonderful spirits and the beautiful prayers they offered.

I have had several spiritual experiences. I hesitate to relate them, as they are sacred to me. However, I will say that the night our daughter, Marilyn was born (November 14, 1925), I saw my father at the foot of my bed. He had been dead two years. As I came out of the anesthetic, I saw him very clearly, and I am sure I was not thinking of him at that time. I always felt that he accompanied her to this earth.

In December, 1945, word got around that President Horace A. Hess was going to be released as president of Yellowstone Stake. Somehow I felt that my husband would succeed him. It seemed that my mother, who was also dead, was constantly near me trying to convey some message to me. I worried a great deal about this. I found myself on my knees asking the Lord to aid the General Authorities, Elder Mark E. Petersen and Elder Matthew Cowley, in choosing the right man as stake president.

Later, when my husband was very ill, Elder Harold B. Lee came to our home to give him a blessing. After the administration, Brother Lee turned to me and said it was made known to him during the prayer that Brother Lewis was the right man for the position.

I have a testimony of this gospel; I know it is true. I only hope I will remain true and steadfast to the end.

Elsie Roberts Lewis
October, 1987

ON THE LORD'S ERRAND

Sunday evenings are special—a time to relax, study the gospel, and reflect on spiritual things. One Sunday evening several years ago, our children were bathed and in their pajamas. The younger ones were already in bed and the older children were getting ready to go.

While earning a nursing degree at Ricks College, my wife was working part-time as a nurse's aide at Madison Memorial Hospital. This summer evening, Julie was completing the two-to-ten shift. Dressed in my pajamas, I was sitting comfortably in the living room reading a favorite book. The stereo played softly in the background.

In this quiet, peaceful hour before Julie would return from work, the thought entered my mind that I ought to get dressed and drive to the hospital to give her a ride home. "But that's silly," I said to myself, since the rear entrance of the hospital was only a two-minute walk through a vacant field to our front door.

I turned the page to read on, but it became difficult to concentrate. The thought returned to put aside the book and music, get dressed, and go to the hospital, even though Julie had at least an hour before quitting time. I reminded myself that I was ready for bed, it was the end of a peaceful Sabbath day, and, besides Julie enjoyed walking home in the fresh air after an eight-hour shift inside the hospital. Finally, I decided it would be easier to dress and drive to the hospital than argue with the nudgings of the Spirit.

Since the main entrance was locked after visiting hours, I went in through the Emergency Room entrance. There I passed one or two doctors, several nurses, and a few patients waiting to see a doctor or pick up a prescription. As I walked to the nurse's station in "A" Wing, I noticed in the blur of activity our local mortician sitting with an elderly, white-haired lady I did not recognize. He held a note pad and pen as he spoke with her.

At the nurse's station, my wife was puzzled to see me, and I felt a little strange being there at that hour. Groping for conversation, I asked if a patient had just died. Julie and several nurses who overheard me nodded silently. Julie explained that an older couple from Pennsylvania had been driving through Rexburg toward home. When the husband suddenly became ill, they turned off the freeway and checked into the nearest motel. His condition worsened, and his wife called an ambulance. He died from cardiac arrest shortly after his arrival at the hospital at approximately the same time my ability to concentrate on my book gave way to the impression to go to the hospital.

Suddenly I realized why I was needed there. With no explanation, I told Julie to meet me in the foyer nearest the Emergency Room when she was ready to leave. I immediately turned and walked to the little, white-haired lady. She was stunned and confused by this shattering event in a strange community so far from home.

"Are you the lady whose husband just passed away?" I asked. She nodded. "What will you do now? Surely you cannot spend the night alone in the motel after what has happened!" I invited her to spend the night with us and decide what to do in the morning, but she did not want to impose on a stranger.

By this time, Julie came down the hall, ready to go home. I introduced her to Mrs. Croisdale and suggested that she might be coming home with us. Garth Flamm, owner of the mortuary and a good friend, said, "Julie, you have four children waiting for you at home, and you are probably exhausted from working an eight-hour shift." With concern for us as well as Mrs. Croisdale, he suggested that the two of us take her to the motel and stay with her until arrangements were made for her husband. He thought he could find a woman in his neighborhood with less responsibility who would spend the night with her.

We then drove to the motel. As I drove into the parking lot and parked, I asked her for the room key. Memories from many years before of our eldest son's death from Sudden Infant Death Syndrome (crib death) came flooding back. How painful it was after Christopher's body had been taken away to see the empty crib and other vivid reminders of his presence with us such a short time before.

Quickly, I opened the room and went in to do what might be necessary before Julie and our lonely friend had time to come inside. Julie sensed what I was thinking and took time to help Mrs. Croisdale out of our van and into the motel. The room was a mess! The EMT's had pulled the man's clothing off and thrown it out of the way to perform CPR. The mattress had been torn from the bed; the blankets and spread were in a heap. But by the time Julie and Mrs. Croisdale approached the door, I had pushed the mattress onto the center of the bed, smoothed out most of the covers, folded his clothing neatly, and placed it on the counter in the bathroom out of sight. Just as I heard their voices, I spotted the man's dentures on the night stand. I picked them up and dropped them into my pocket.

Julie came into the room with one arm around the dear lady, consoling her. When Julie saw the outline of the dentures in my pocket, she pulled me aside and whispered, "Go to the mortuary, find Garth, and give these to him immediately!" (Living with a nurse has taught me that when someone dies, his false teeth must be placed in his mouth soon, or it will be impossible later on.)

When I returned from my errand, Garth Flamm's bishop arrived with one of his ward members, an older widow, who could comfort Mrs. Croisdale in her grief. What my wife and I did to help this stranger in her darkest hour required little effort, but to this helpless woman, alone and so far from home, it was important indeed.

As we were leaving, the little lady who had checked into that motel room a few hours earlier with her husband, held out her arms to embrace us. She was unable to say anything, but the tears we all shed were profound expressions of what we felt so deeply. As I held her briefly and looked into those grief-stricken eyes, I was so grateful I had responded to the Spirit and driven to the hospital that Sunday evening. When she kissed me on the cheek, I knew I had been *on the Lord's errand*.

Darwin Wolford
March, 1987

MY TESTIMONY
OF HOME EVENING

Family home evening is an important tradition in our home. How thankful I am as a mother for a night that we can count on being together as a family. Monday night is very sacred in our home, because it is *our* night. Some home evenings are not as rewarding or outstanding as others, but the time is still ours.

I gained a deep and abiding testimony of the importance of home evening from an incident that happened to our family a few years ago. Like a lot of other families, we have found home evening a good time to discuss important family matters. At the time of this particular home evening, our family consisted of Brian, who had just turned five; Kathy, soon to be four; Kevin a little over two. We were expecting a fourth baby within a couple of weeks.

We hadn't yet discussed as a family the new baby because the children were young and we wanted to treat the matter as sacredly as we could. Brent, my husband, started our home evening that night with the little ones around him. He said we were going to talk about something very special. He turned to our oldest and asked, "Brian, where were you when Mama and Daddy lived in Salt Lake?" Brian thought a moment and then replied, "Oh, I was up in heaven getting finished. You know, getting my eyes and ears and things." His dad said that was probably right and then we went on to tell him about how excited we were when we knew that we were going to have him and why his name is so special. Brian then showed the pictures in the picture album of when he was blessed, when he came home from the hospital, when he learned to walk, and so on.

All the time the other two children were exclaiming, "And then I was borned," and then I was borned, wasn't I!" We then told Kathy how excited we were when we found out that we were going to have her. She followed by quickly telling us that she had been in heaven taking care of her brother, Kevin.

We looked at pictures of Kathy and talked about her name, discussing why she had the name she had. Kevin could hardly wait for his turn, and we did the same thing with him.

Brent then told them that Heavenly Father was sending another spirit to our home just as he had sent them, and it wouldn't be too long before this baby would be born. Kathy immediately jumped up and danced around the room, her pink nightgown twirling, shouting, "My little sister, she's coming, she's coming." Then she stopped abruptly and said, "How do you know, Mom?" We then went into a little detail—as much as we felt they needed—with my husband concluding that, "This is a time when we especially need Heavenly Father's help so that Mama and our baby will be blessed." He then admonished them to always remember them in their prayers.

After that, our little ones never needed to be reminded to ask Heavenly Father to bless us that our baby would be born safely and that Mama would be all right.

They greeted that new little one (Kathy got her sister) with such enthusiasm we could hardly keep them away from Kristen Gai. From the time she was born they loved her and played with her so sweetly. There was never resentment or wishing we didn't have the baby.

Just fifteen months later we gathered these same children around us in another home evening and began to talk about this little sister again, explaining that the next day would be her funeral. She had drowned the Saturday before on June 9, 1973—two hours after the birth of our fifth child, Kyle. The children really didn't know what had happened to her. They had not yet seen her body. They just knew she wasn't home.

As we explained what had happened—that they would be seeing just her body in her casket; that her spirit, that part of her that made her laugh and smile and play had gone to be with Heaveny Father—the sweetest, most peaceful Spirit came into our home. We were inspired to tell the children that we felt they were very special brothers and sisters and that Heavenly Father had always known that Kristen wouldn't be able to be on this earth very long, so he had sent her to a home where her brothers and sisters would really love her and make her limited earth life very special for her. We talked about how she would always be a part of our family, but that she just wouldn't be here with us.

Today, our children talk about death very comfortably. They tell their younger brothers and sisters (we have since had three more sons and two more daughters: Matt, Layne, Janeen, Karen, and Michael) about their other sister and how wonderful it will be when we can all be together again as a family.

I testify that we could not have handled the situation as parents if we had not been having home evening and if we had not been in the habit of discussing spiritual things with our children. I know that our Heavenly Father will inspire us to handle situations as they occur in our homes and lives if we will try to keep in tune spiritually and do those things we've been asked and that the opportunity is there for us to be together through the eternities, as we qualify ourselves accordingly.

Donna Jean Kinghorn
May, 1985

THE LOST STONE

On January 20, 1987, after about a week and a half with an agonizing toothache, I finally visited the dentist. We were living in Vidor, Texas. As he surveyed the damage and began quoting my options and his price to save the tooth, I became resigned to the idea of just having it pulled. I knew that relief would be immediate this way and the cost much less.

After the extraction, I came home, propped up my feet, and was preparing to be waited upon by my family, when the phone rang. My husband, Randal, was calling to remind me of the obligation one of us had to serve that evening at the data entry center at a neighboring stake center about thirty miles away. We took turns every week. It was actually his turn to go, but our boys had a basketball game that night. Since Randal hadn't been able to see any of their games yet, I had offered to take his place.

For a moment I considered calling the supervisor to explain my very recent "minor surgery" only 45 minutes earlier and say I would be unable to go. I felt that I had a valid reason, but then came a little thought reminding me of the commitment we had made to this calling. Besides, I was having remarkably little pain.

We gathered our children together right before my ride came to give them last-minute instructions and explain to them the things that needed to be completed before the game: dinner preparation, homework, piano practice, dishes, etc. As I was discussing a homework question with our son, Nolan, I happened to glance at my left hand after it caught on the fabric of the couch. To my horror, the main stone was missing from my wedding ring. I sat staring at it, but only for a moment. Then I began frantically searching for the stone. It had been loose for awhile, and I had been aware that it needed to be tightened, so I really deserved this lesson. As I walked to my room to put the ring in my jewelry box, I felt a tear fall, knowing it would be a long time before a new stone could be purchased and the ring repaired, for money was scarce at our house.

Since this special token of love had been part of my attire for nearly fifteen years, I was very upset. Two minutes remained in which to search before my ride came, but the stone never turned up.

With gauze still adorning my upper lip, I climbed into the car, lamenting my recent loss. The worry I felt never completely left my mind, nor did I cease silently praying, even when I was engrossed in typing names from family group sheets into the computer at the data entry center. Then an amazing thing happend. I came across a problem that even my supervisor couldn't work through, so I went to find one of the main directors. I located her at a Scout meeting, and she soon explained how to handle the problem. I returned to my work, and as I was relating her instructions to my supervisor, I pushed my hands into the pockets of my jeans, a habit of mine while speaking. I felt what seemed to be a small rock among the lint in my right pocket. I was about to drop the rock into the trash can, when in astonishment, I realized that it was the stone to my ring. I stared at my hand and again felt tears spilling over, but this time they were tears of gratitude and wonder.

How did that stone get into my *right* pocket? There was no logical explanation. I attempted to reach my left hand that would have had my ring on it around to put it into the right pocket of my jeans, but couldn't comfortably do so. I reasoned that the stone could not have dropped out of the ring into my pocket since my left hand could never have reached it. There was no way this could have happened naturally.

When I sat down to type again, I had a very warm feeling inside. I knew that it wasn't just by chance that the stone had been found and in such a peculiar place. To me this was a special blessing from my Heavenly Father. Since I was where I was supposed to be, doing his work, and didn't use pain and fatigue as an excuse to not do this important work, he had rewarded me for being faithful. I felt a special closeness to him that night and knew the people on the other side of the veil were nearby. I knew for a surety that evening that he loved *me* and had answered my humble prayer.

I testify that all the work we do in the Church, no matter how insignificant we may feel it is, makes a difference to the kingdom, and we will be blessed for our efforts if we are committed and willingly serve.

Wendy Bradford Wright
September, 1987

DON'T QUIT

My parents, Robert and Dorothy Wilding Fenton, joyfully greeted their children as we each in turn blessed their home. I was fourth in this grand family of four sons and five daughters, arriving November 17, 1956, through the efforts of Dr. Blaine Passey. I weighed seven pounds and two ounces.

All concerned were happy, yet fearful. I was born with a rare birth defect called spina bifida. A vertebrae had not fully developed, leaving a protruding spinal cord leaking spinal fluid. It looked like an open sore the size of a dollar and an inch high. Local and area doctors came, showing great interest in my case. It was the first one known to occur in the old hospital at Rexburg, Idaho, except for a similar one of Dr. Harlo Rigby's. The infant had died.

The following day, I was given the name of Michael Ray Fenton and a father's blessing by my father and Bishop Charles Hamilton, of Sugar City, Idaho.

Bishop Hamilton told my parents to have faith and everything would be all right. Leaving my angel mother in the hospital, Dad, accompanied by Grandma Mahalia Wilding, went with me to the Primary Children's Hospital in Salt Lake City, Utah. I was only five days old when Dr. Charles A. Powell, a specialist in this field, performed a very delicate operation. Using special electrical instruments, he found the nerves and muscles that would indicate which area to cut to put my spinal cord back in place. To this day I have no bone in that area. Dr. Powell cautioned, "Don't be too hopeful. There's a possibility Michael will never walk."

After a week, I was released and returned home to my mother. With love, faith, and prayers, my parents nursed me. This was difficult, because for six weeks I had to lie with a sand pillow under my stomach to allow the sore to heal without complications. No one could pick me up. I could wear only an undershirt, and no coverings were advised.

A cardboard box with an opening in one end was placed over my basket with a warm light bulb in it to keep me cozy and secure. I had no feeling from my waist down. My recovery was truly amazing.

On February 13, 1957, Elder John Longden, an Assistant to the Quorum of the Twelve, came to our home and gave me a special priesthood blessing. He was attending stake conference in the area and willingly responded to my parents' request. In the blessing, among other things, he said, "You will be able to walk." This wonderful pronouncement was fulfilled when I was two years and two months old. As I grew, I gained feeling in my legs and feet. I used crutches, and they continue to be my dependable "helpers."

Several challenging, but not surprising incidents have subsequently occurred. For exampe: At eight, I broke both legs when I fell off a bicycle my brother, Bruce, was pedaling. My casts didn't keep me down. I became accustomed to a stroller, and my dad took me fishing. With the pole and worms in my hands, I often caught my limit.

Bruce pumped me on the bike to school in the fall and spring. In winter, he pulled me on a sled. Each day, using my crutches, I went to my grandparents' for lunch. They lived next to the Sugar City School where I attended the first and second grades. One day I spent my whole lunch hour getting there. The pathway was filled with deep snow. I took one step, fell down, got up, and tried again. Finally, Mother saw me from the window and came to my aid.

How I enjoyed baseball at age ten with my schoolmates and neighborhood friends. I pitched. When my team was up to bat, I hit the ball and someone else ran for me.

During my eleventh summer, both my ankles had to be stabilized because I couldn't bend them. This caused my feet to drag when I walked. The operation was performed in the LDS Hospital at Idaho Falls by Dr. Boge. As soon as I could walk, I was transferred to the Elk's Rehabilitation Center at Boise, Idaho, where I was given special exercises and treatments to strengthen my ankles.

At this center, I developed a lasting friendship with Terry Whittier. He had a defect termed short cords. He was full of energy and often impressed me with his wheelchair antics. We both walked with crutches. Later I enjoyed him at Ricks College in Rexburg.

Twelve was a highlight for me as I was ordained a deacon in the Aaronic Priesthood and was asked to be president of the quorum. I felt it an honor to pass the sacrament to the congregation. I held the trays in my right hand and a crutch in my left.

In my youth, Mother encouraged me to take piano lessons. In 1976, after the Teton Dam flood, we moved to St. Anthony, Idaho, where we attended church in the Twin Groves Ward. Bishop Grant Bischoff asked me to serve as ward organist. I could play the piano, but not the organ. Mother arranged for me to take organ lessons from Sister Janet Mortensen. I had limited feeling in my feet, yet felt I could play the organ. With prayer, faith, effort, and a lot of encouragement from my teacher, I learned. I have been organist for priesthood meetings, a ward organist at Ricks College, and have held several music positions.

School was enjoyable for me because teachers and students were considerate and helpful. I shall always be grateful to them. It was a good experience to be president of my ninth grade sminary class, even though I broke a leg that year. At school I had to hop up four flights of stairs. During my junior year in high school, I received the "I Dare You" award, given to one student who portrayed a willingness to strive more diligently. Those grand students and teachers gave me a standing ovation.

When they were nineteen, several of my buddies headed for the mission field. At that age, I, too, desired to serve my Heavenly Father, but, due to another operation on my feet, was forced to wait. I attended Ricks College one semester and then went to the Eastern Idaho Vocation Technical School at Idaho Falls for two years. In 1980, I obtained a position as a teller at the Valley Bank in St. Anthony.

I still yearned to fulfill a two-year mission. I filled out the necessary papers and anxiously waited for a call. I was turned down. Disappointment filled my soul, yet I didn't give up. Fortunately, the Church commenced allowing missionaries to serve for a six-month or one-year period. My good friend, Terry Whittier, who was attending Ricks College, received his call to the Idaho Boise Mission. He said, "Mike, why don't you go on a mission, too? With the new program, you can go. All you need to do is contact your stake president."

In 1982, I talked to Bishop Bischoff and our stake president, Neil L. Kunz. President Kunz made arrangements, and I was soon called to serve for one year in the Idaho Boise Mission.

At this time, Dad was acquainted with Johnny Pierson of Rexburg. He had been in an accident which paralyzed his legs. Johnny is unusually mechanically minded. He built a mechanical device for his car that enabled him to operate the brake and gas pedal with a lever on the steering column. We went to see him. What an uplift this proved to be. He made a device for me to use on a car I'd purchased. When my mission call came, I was given permission to take my car to alleviate some of the walking to proselyte.

Instead of serving in the mission office as I'd expected, President John K. Carmack was inspired to send me out as a proselyting missionary. My first area was Meridian, Idaho, and my companion was Elder Curry. Some trials and many choice experiences strengthened my testimony.

President Carmack gave me a priesthood blessing. He said, "Someday you will find a companion to be your wife." I didn't expect such a promise to be fulfilled in this life and thought little more about it. At my release, President Carmack was called to serve as a General Authority in the First Quorum of the Seventy. (It is interesting to note that after I was released, the Church's mission length policy was changed back to two years.)

In the fall of 1984, I enrolled again at Ricks College. I became involved in a group called Ricks Outdoor Cooperative Handicap Association (R.O.C.H.A.). I enjoyed many great adventures, including snow skiing, rapelling, overnight camping, nature hikes, fishing, dog sledding, and scuba diving.

I took two years of secretarial and business courses. Through my roommate, the first year I met Angela Faulkner from upstate New York. She returned the second year. Just before Homecoming, Angela and I talked about the upcoming big dance. It was girls' choice. I accepted her invitation!

On April 17, 1986, we graduated from Ricks and were married the following day in the Logan Temple in Utah. The celestial ceremony, uniting us for time and all eternity, was performed by my former mission president, Elder John K. Carmack. Our parents and many other faithful loved ones and friends joined with us to show their love. I'm deeply grateful for Angela, such a beloved partner, helpmate, and eternal companion. She brings untold joy and happiness to me. My parents and family have been a constant strength with their love, support, and understanding. They are incredible.

I cherish my fervent testimony of the truthfulness of the restored gospel of Jesus Christ. Humbly, I acknowledge the gifts, power, and marvelous blessings of the priesthood of God and also the many prayers he has answered in my behalf. At times, life is extremely difficult for me. Nonetheless, I have always felt greatly loved and blessed by our Heavenly Father. Trials and problems have helped me develop unwavering faith in his word and become strong in body and spirit. I have developed a slogan which has helped and encouraged me when things looked discouraging: "Don't Quit." Throughout my life, this slogan has had a definite and remarkable influence on me. I sincerely pray that none of us will ever give up or quit in the effort to make the most of ourselves.

Michael Ray Fenton

Compiler's Note: Elder John K. Carmack, Michael Fenton's former mission president, made the following statement regarding Elder Fenton.

I first recall hearing the name, Michael Fenton, when a copy of a letter sent to him by the Missionary Department of the Church was sent to me suggesting that he get in touch with the Idaho Boise Mission president, President John K. Carmack, who might be able to use him in the Idaho Boise Mission.

In consulting with President Kunz, Michael was issued a call to serve a full-time stake mission within the Idaho Boise Mission. We arranged for him to come to Boise as all other missionaries do, to be trained and briefed there, to be sent out and trained by a regular missionary, and to serve in every way as a full-time missionary. Elder Fenton brought as fine a spirit as we ever had into the mission field. We gave him no special consideration. We even sent him to work in an area which required him to walk a flight of stairs to get into his apartment. We knew this would be difficult, but we had agreed with him and with his stake president that he would serve without special consideration, enduring the same hardships and sacrifices as other missionaries.

No words can express the love and respect Sister Carmack and I have for Elder Fenton. He never asked for a single special favor in his missionary work. He served faithfully, was most effective in touching the hearts and lives of many people, and had the full love and respect of all his companions. I remember how much love and respect one of his investigators, Reverend Wally Cooper, had for Elder Fenton, although he has not joined the Church thus far to my knowledge. Elder Fenton's testimonies in zone conference, his struggles to learn the discussions and the scriptures, and his willingness to overcome his handicaps will always remain a vivid memory and highlight of our mission experience.

It was a perfect delight to meet Michael's lovely wife, Angela. It was my privilege to perform their sealing for time and all eternity in the Logan Temple. I have never felt a stronger witness of the Holy Ghost than I did on that day. Many of his and Angela's friends were present. They are an oustanding couple with great determination. Elder Fenton has truly blessed the lives of the missionaries with whom he served in the Idaho Boise Mission.

THE LORD GIVETH,
AND THE LORD TAKETH AWAY

Our five-year-old, Catherine, the youngest of our three children, was run over in a tragic bus accident on Friday, March 15, 1985. She was returning from kindergarten at the time, walking across the street in front of the school bus about one and a half blocks from our home.

It was difficult for us to accept the reality of Catherine's death. My wife, Lynn; Catherine's brothers, Christopher, eleven, and Courtney, nine and a half; and I were haunted by the "what ifs." This caused a big void in our lives.

The day of her accident things had gone exceptionally well. I had taken ther day off to attend the state basketball tournament. Only two hours before, I had visited Catherine in her kindergarten class. She was happy to see me and behaved well. She reminded me, "Daddy, be sure to pick me up early from the babysitter's 'cause you said we'd all go to the game."

I had a lot of admiration for her patient and thoughtful teacher. Since it was close to St. Patrick's Day, she and the children were engrossed in making an Irish stew, believed by the Irish to keep evil spirits away. Catherine was pleased and proud to peal potatoes for it.

This was a feat she'd often done at home. Lynn made a lot of her clothes; how adorable she looked in them.

Following the accident, Catherine was taken to a hospital. We didn't have time nor could we get close enough to give her a priesthood blessing. She lived possibly thirty minutes, but her heart didn't beat and she didn't breathe on her own.

The immediate response of caring relatives, friends, our bishopric, ward members, students, and teachers (especially from Friday through Sunday) was touching. Their love and compassion eased our pain and disappointment. We cannot adequately thank them.

We knew our feelings and reactions at losing Catherine were natural. We wanted our little sweetheart to remain with us *now* and not have to wait for celestial glory to again be together. It was our option to be bitter or to count our many blessings. "The Lord gave, and the Lord hath taken away; blessed be the name of the Lord" (Job 1:21). We vowed to accept his will.

Catherine looked forward to being "babitized" (as she would say), when she was eight years old. She was five when we went as a family to Courtney's baptism. This necessary and special ordinance impressed her. We had taught her that our Savior, Jesus Christ, had set this example for us, as had her brothers.

Early in the morning of June 12, 1985, we received a remarkable, sustaining blessing. A person telephoned saying that he had a three-hour-old baby boy we could adopt. He needed our decision by 8:00 a.m. the same day. Naturally, we returned his call within minutes. "We want the baby boy."

We picked him up the next day. From then on, we called him Clark. The person who called us said he knew of twenty-five to thirty other people who were waiting to adopt a child, but he could only think of us and that he wanted us to have this opportunity.

A few days later, we visited with my wife's sister who related a dream she had recently had. She said, "There are two more children for you to adopt."

Clark fits perfectly into our family. We know Catherine had something to do with this adoption. We feel certain she is helping us find a little girl to adopt. Through our faith, fasting, and prayers, this will come to pass.

Lynn and I cherish each other and our wonderful children. We are humbly grateful for the strength and encouragement received daily through kneeling together in family prayer. At these precious times, we acknowledge the numerous blessings Heavenly Father bestows, often through the love and support of others. We pray for our needs, thanking him for the restored gospel and its guidance, and for his assurance that there is plan and purpose in this world and in our lives. May we ever strive to pass this awesome earthly test and in time merit being an eternal family.

O'Dell Peterson

FAIRYTALES STILL COME TRUE

Every girl dreams of meeting her "Prince Charming" in a romantic way, like Cinderella or Snow White did. That is why Bob and I call our meeting an "LDS Fairytale."

On a crisp, April 6th morning in 1962, at Provo, Utah, I climbed the BYU campus steps and soon thereafter boarded a bus with 500 other students to sing at the Friday session of the LDS general conference in the famous Salt Lake Tabernacle. I was feeling low from study pressures and felt very lonely. Dating, even at BYU among thousands of men and many returned missionaries, had been discouraging, too. The young men I wanted to date didn't ask me, and those who did weren't to my liking. I had prayed to the Lord many times to help me find the one companion in the world who would be best suited for me. I had given up on dating; my self-esteem was at a low ebb.

Upon arriving at the west side of the Tabernacle, we hurried inside to take our places in the choir seats. Just being in this marvelous building with its renowned acoustical properties brought a warm feeling to me. Near the 10:00 hour for conference to convene, the General Authorities took their seats and with them was President David O. McKay, with his imposing white hair. As I watched him, my bosom swelled and tears came to my eyes and streamed down my face. I knew he was a prophet of God. That special feeling of awe and gratitude made me want to sing with all my heart.

Unknown to me, there was a recently returned missionary in the audience named Bob Webster. He was a convert of nearly four years and had come with his bishop to serve as an usher and to be spiritually renewed. Prior to his mission to Uruguay, he had been a Tabernacle usher at general conference with Joe Sturdy, a man who was instrumental in his conversion. Upon his mission release in late July, 1962, he had enrolled at Cal Poly at Pomona, California, and wasn't able to attend October conference. It was a special blessing for him to be there this April with his bishop and other friends.

At this time in Bob's life, the girls he had dated didn't seem spiritually right to him. In frustration, he had decided to forget dating and let the Lord find him the companion referred to in his patriarchal blessing.

At conference, while ushering at the morning session, Bob looked over the BYU chorus. Thoughts of his wonderful year at BYU after joining the Church flooded his mind. Suddenly a girl with a long, dark ponytail attracted him. She was dressed modestly, attentive to the conductor (not flirting or whispering as some were), and she seemed thrilled with President McKay's presence. It seemed she put her whole heart into her singing, like an angel from heaven's chorus. He was deeply impressed with her in many ways. His friend, Joe, suuggested that he get acquainted with this young lady right after conference. Bob liked the idea.

While I was standing outside the choir entrance following the conference session, two young men approached me, shook my hand warmly and introduced themselves as Joe Sturdy and Aksel Tanner. "Oh, no," I thought. Here are a couple of fellows looking for an LDS girl to date."

They were polite and friendly, easy to talk to, and they soon explained that they had a friend they wanted me to meet. Subsequently, a tall, clean-cut, returned-missionary type young man came around the corner, and they introduced him as Bob Webster. My attention was not drawn to his appearance especially, but was focused more on what they wanted and why they were talking to me. Our conversation turned to Bob's mission. We discovered that a lady in my ward had also gone to Uruguay on a mission, and Bob knew her. I agreed to contact her for him and get information about his missionary reunion to be held soon, in which case he needed my phone number. It was not my habit to give it freely.

Weary from the excitement of the day and lack of sleep, I told them good-bye and went by bus to my parent's home in Salt Lake, not thinking any more about the meeting. At home, I was told that Bob had called. He soon called again and said he had found his reunion information. Then he invited me to go with him. I felt uneasy about going with a stranger. Also, I had a roommate with me that I didn't want to leave alone. I explained the situation and added, "If you can find someone to go with my roommate, it might work out." He could think of one possibility, a missionary who had returned with him from his mission. When he told me his name, I recognized it as the name of the office manager at the store where I had worked the previous summer. Some coincidence. The double date was arranged.

Dating had often left me feeling uneasy and self-conscious. However, I felt very much at ease with Bob that evening, even with a totally foreign group of people and listening to Spanish I didn't understand. He was very gracious in his introductions and I immediately felt a part of his enthusiasm while greeting his friends and new aquaintances. On the way home, Bob said he would like me to come to Joe's home and see slides of his mission the following evening.

They came for me, and we went to Joe's, but we didn't see Bob's slides. To his chagrin the projector broke down, not once, but twice. We enjoyed visiting with Joe and his family, after which Bob took me home. The two of us talked and talked, all night in fact, until 5:00 a.m. getting acquainted.

As we watched the snowflakes softly fall outside the car, it dawned on me that Bob was going to his home 700 miles away. One of the conference speakers had talked about fasting and prayer. It struck Bob so clearly that if he wanted to find out quickly from the Lord if I were meant for him that he could know by fasting and prayer. He began to fast right then. When Bob felt the time was right, he said, "I wanted to know if you were the right one for me, Donna, so I have been fasting about you."

The thought hit me strongly, "What little faith you have, Donna. If you want to know about Bob, you, too, need to fast." There was no second guessing. I knew it was the thing to do, and I had faith from previous experience that the Lord answers prayers.

As we walked to my door, Bob asked me to pray with him. I had never done that before with a date. I recalled my bishop saying that a couple should pray together to see if they were meant for each other. We knelt by a big chair in the living room. My roommate was sleeping soundly on a couch nearby. Bob offered such a simple, beautiful prayer that I was touched.

After returning to Joe's home that morning, Bob decided that his fast had been sufficient and he ate breakfast. He wondered to himself, "What kind of a crazy weekend romance is this? It all seems so fast and foolish."

He told me later that he had almost regretted looking me in the eye again when he picked me up for the Sunday morning conference session. Yet, when he came for me and I opened the door, he was overwhelmed by the conviction that he was looking at his future wife. "I felt like we already belonged to each other," he said.

Now back in the Tabernacle, Bob ushered. He told me he felt numb with love, not to mention lack of sleep. He mentioned to his stake president, bishop, Joe, and Aksel, and several others, that he had found his wife. He knew it was by the power of the Holy Ghost. Never had a testimony engulfed him with such surety. He couldn't doubt. He knew. The thought of having such a person love him completely was almost too much for him to stand. To meet her on April 6th, to know by the Spirit, and to ask her hand on the Sabbath made the perfect LDS Fairytale.

During conference, I couldn't keep from looking at Bob the whole time. "Could this really be happening to me?" I thought. "It is impossible to love someone so much and for him to love me equally."

Following the session, we walked to his car to talk. Only forty-four hours had passed since we first met, and he had asked me to be his wife. I was stunned and scared. Discouragement came quickly as my fears surfaced. Bob left, feeling dejected. I wept on my way home, knowing Bob was returning to California. I feared that he would never write or see me again.

I confided in my mother. Her gentle, wise counsel was, "Don't do anything rash but be patient." She had always been understandng, not interfering when she felt I had things under control.

As I returned to Provo that night to resume college, I was tired, humbled, and confused. I knelt by my bed before retiring and opened my whole soul to the Lord and asked for assurance to know if Bob was right for me. A calm, beautiful feeling came over me. My bosom swelled until I thought it would burst.

Again the next morning I prayed. The same feeling came and lifted me up until I felt as if I were floating along. The Holy Ghost had borne testimony to me that Bob and I should marry. I didn't waste any time in writing a letter to him that day, but I didn't have the courage to mail it for fear he might have rejected me. I saw his friend, Aksel, on campus and asked if I could talk to him. His words were comforting and he told me all he knew about Bob and what kind of a person he was.

When I returned to my apartment, a letter from Bob was waiting. He had written it on his way home to reassure me that he knew what the Lord had told him was right and the Lord would also help me know for sure. His letter took away my fears and I mailed my letter to him. But I already had my answer.

Was it easy sailing from there? Have you ever tried to tell someone about a three-day engagement? Skepticism often came our way from those who didn't understand the source of our decision, but we knew and that gave us strength to prepare for the most important event of our lives, marriage.

Two weekends later, Bob drove to Provo from California so we could make our September wedding plans. We corresponded frequently. The pieces of the puzzle fell together as we discovered our compatibility in music, Spanish, sports, major lifetime goals, and ideals. Our birthdays were only one day apart. Ironically, we answered each other's questions in letters that crossed in the mail before they were received. We were married and sealed in the Logan Utah Temple for time and eternity on September 20, 1962.

Twenty-three years and nine children later, (six sons and three daughters), we're still working at married life. Yes, I mean working at it. Marriage may have been quick and easy, but staying married is an eternal process. We have been through college, financial depression, health problems, difference, of opinion, middle-age crises, and child rearing. At times I have wondered if our marriage will survive, but underneath there is one thing for sure. We know God ordained our marriage, and it is up to us to make it endure to the end and get better along the way so it can be celestial.

We know that God hears and answers our prayers. Any person who desires to know can ask God and receive an answer, especially when it comes to the biggest decision in life, celestial marriage. We know he hears and answers our prayers daily and those of our children, too. We're grateful that he is there to guide them and us as we each strive to live the beautiful teachings of the gospel of Jesus Christ.

Donna Webster
June, 1985

"GOD HATH NOT PROMISED SKIES ALWAYS BLUE"

When Vernall was born to my husband, Morris, and me, on May 27, 1933, he was our second child, our firstborn being Keith. (Morris had a son who died in infancy, and a daughter, LaFay, by his former wife.) Following Vernall, four more children joined our family: Gary, Darrell, Dorothy, and Sharon.

In 1939, at five and a half, Vernall had rheumatic fever. The miracle drugs of today were not available and knowledge to treat victims was limited. His heart became badly damaged. As a result, he suffered and had to be in bed more than he was up. Out of twenty-nine years, he spent a considerable portion of twelve years in hospitals.

He required a hospital bed at home, as well as a large oxygen tank, so that I could care for his needs. I learned to give him shots, and ironed hot flannels to apply on his chest to relieve his pain. He was not completely free from heart pain at any time after he was first afflicted. How grateful we were for the intermittent periods when he could be in a wheelchair.

When Vernall's health permitted, he helped teach and take care of his younger brothers and sisters. He was unable to attend school after a few months in the third grade. His keen mind and an ever-increasing desire to learn made it a joy for each family member to assist him, not only with his formal education, but in numerous other ways. As he grew older, he read a lot of excellent books, studied and pondered the scriptrues, and enjoyed LDS Church books.

We always appreciated his jovial nature and felt his constant love, gratitude, and concern for us. He never complained or gave up; his faith in the Lord Jesus Christ and his perseverance and patience were an inspiration, not only to us but to many others.

From 1950 to 1968, Morris and I owned and operated the Tropical Restaurant in Brigham City, Utah. During some brief periods, Vernall was able to act as cashier. He loved doing this and associating with the customers and employees.

In December, 1962, at age twenty-nine, Vernall had heart surgery at the LDS Hospital in Salt Lake City, Utah. He had contacted the Red Cross on his own and made all the necessary arrangements for blood donors and the operation without our knowledge so as not to worry us. LaFay came from Idaho to be with him during and after surgery. We appreciated her support, her husband, Pete Hackworth's, and also the strength and comfort of all our children during this critical time.

Morris had been hospitalized in Ogden, Utah, for several months due to his heart condition, and had only been home a week when Vernall passed away on February 4, 1963, six weeks after surgery. The last time I saw Vernall, I kissed him before leaving his room. He gave me a look I will never forget. He didn't want me to leave him.

While I was returning home to Brigham City, a hospital attendant called our home. Morris answered and said in unbelief, "It cannot be. My wife is with Vernall." Upon arriving in our driveway, I learned the sad news. Although we had felt our son's death was imminent, it was a shock. We rushed back to the hospital, but Vernall was gone. His doctors said a much higher power than theirs had spared his life for at least fourteen years longer than they had anticipated he could possibly live. An autopsy revealed that his heart had been eaten like a sieve because of intense, uncontrolled fevers of 104 degrees to 106 degrees for long periods of time.

We are humbly aware that Heavenly Father gave us and our family the wisdom and strength to take care of Vernall. We feel he is happy and continuing to progress. We know that if each of us endures faithfully and is obedient to God's laws and ordinances, we will be with Vernall. It is a great comfort to us that his temple work has been done.

Between 1972 and 1974, Morris was hospitalized several times due to heart attacks. Before he had heart surgery in February, 1974, he came very close to death. His son who died in infancy came to him at that time with a message. He told Morris he could die or remain to finish his earthly mission. The baby didn't speak, but Morris understood his message. When Morris decided to come back, the baby's eyes glistened like star in approval.

Eleven surgeons discussed Morris' case and concluded surgery would be very risky. Both his surgeon and cardiologist told them, "You don't know this man like we do; he needs this chance to fight for his life."

The surgeon told Morris, "I cannot make you any promises." Morris smiled and replied, "I know I will make it. Let's get started." Like Vernall, he was a fighter.

He was in surgery eight and one-half hours. His heart was removed and attached to a machine that breathed for him and did all the marvelous work his heart did. Arteries were removed from both his legs and used to replace three main arteries in his heart. The doctors and I were amazed at his subsequent recovery.

Since then he has suffered much heart and angina pain, but we are very thankful to all who had anything to do with his care, and especially to Heavenly Father for extending his life. It has been a great blessing for Morris and me to work together in business for many years and for both of us to serve in various Church positions throughout our married lives, as well as to do some temple work. It has been a privilege to rear our children, to watch our posterity grow and achieve.

My dear companion and sweetheart for fifty-seven years (we were married October 4, 1929), passed away March 27, 1987, from congestive heart failure, in Everett, Washington, where we have resided for several years. His lovely memorial services and interment were four days later at Brigham City. Due to my health problems, I was unable to attend, but I could visualize my eternal companion clothed in the robes of the temple, and in my thoughts I was with our family, loved ones, and friends who came far and near to show their love and respect. I could see the peaceful place for Morris' grave near Vernall's and contemplated the meaning of the gift of resurrection.

Even though "God hath not promised skies always blue," I know he continually grants us faith, strength, and serenity to weather the storms. He has promised us a greater blessing, a higher path of assistance, than merely preventing pain and sorrow. His promise is that with his help and the beautiful plan of life and exaltation, we can rise above our afflictions and each day grow within.

Dorothy Arbon Nuttall
August, 1987

ONE SMALL MOMENT
CHANGED MY LIFE

Although I've never had a dramatic change or experienced a "bolt of lightning" in my life, I want to share a small moment that has had a great impact on me and given my life direction.

At the age of eleven, I was placed in the Belmont County Children's Home in Cambridge, Ohio. It was by far the biggest "house" I had ever seen. Since everyone had to work, I was assigned to mop a long hallway. The mop closet contained a large, deep sink, several brooms and buckets, and mops of all sizes. The first time I stepped into that closet I was overwhelmed, not just by the sight that met my eyes, but by the feeling in my heart.

How did I get here? What had happened to my mother's promise to take care of me? Somehow, I understood she had done everything in her power to provide for my two-and one-half year-old brother and me. Her poor health and lack of money kept her from taking care of us.

Standing in that mop closet, I suddenly felt an assurance that I had another set of parents with higher intelligence, more power, and greater love than any earthly parent could possess. As a result of that experience, I had the strength to face the world.

And I faced the world for the next five years on my own. Even without a knowledge of God's plan of life and exaltation, my realization that someone cared very much became my guiding light.

I don't know how many rough times I've gone through by hanging on to that single thread of knowledge, but I do know and bear testimony that we can survive anything this earth confronts us with by knowing that our Heavenly Parents do indeed love us and are anxiously awaiting our return.

Betty Lou Stephens Bell
December, 1985

THE FAITH OF LITTLE CHILDREN

I have been the coroner for Fremont County for the past 24 years. During this time I have had several unusual experiences; however, none was more unusual than the one that happened in August, 1968.

I received a phone call from the Idaho State dispatcher that a man had drowned in the Island Park Reservoir and that I was needed. I was to report immediately. The body was at the lake.

I called Sherriff Butts and advised him of the accident. I asked if he would like to ride with me in the ambulance. Besides being coroner, my job was to operate the ambulance. I was a certified ambulance attendant.

Sherrif Butts and I drove from St. Anthony to Island Park with the ambulance lights and siren on, driving at a high rate of speed.

Upon our arrival, a state patrolman escorted us to where the reported drowning had occurred. It was near the McCrea bridge on the inlet to the reservoir.

As I backed up the ambulance, I could see a body covered with a sheet lying near the lakeside. Just as we neared the body, I noticed it was moving! It was an unbelieveable sight. I had never had a case where the victim was still alive when I arrived. As a coroner, I dealt only with dead bodies.

I soon learned that the patient had been revived but was not conscious. Consequently, he was in need of oxygen and the special care that I could provide.

We loaded the patient on the stretcher and put him in the ambulance. I asked Sheriff Butts to drive while I attended to the victim's needs in the back. I invited the victim's wife to ride with us, and we then rushed to the Ashton Memorial Hospital.

While riding and with oxygen being administered, the patient seemed stable. This allowed me to visit with the man's wife. I asked her to relate what had hapened.

She said, "We are an LDS family. This weekend we have been vacationing in Island Park having a great time."

I had noticed five children when I first picked up the body. The children seemed a year or two apart with the eldest eight or nine years old and the youngest, one.

I vividly recall her saying, "The children built a crude raft. They were rafting out in the lake and a motor boat passed by them. The wake from the motor boat caused the raft to capsize and fall apart. They all fell into the lake. My husband, realizing the seriousness of the situation, jumped into the lake and swam to save our children. Of course, they all grabbed hold of good old Dad. Yet he managed to keep them afloat until bystanders along the lake could swim out and take the children to safety. None were wearing lifejackets or at least not sufficient jackets to keep them all afloat. When they looked back for Dad, he was nowhere in sight. Concerned bystanders spent considerable time trying to find him, probably 15 minutes. Finally he was located and brought ashore."

In those days few people knew how to give CPR or mouth-to-mouth resuscitation. She explained that several methods were tried: the old conventional artificial respiration, even raising his arms and dropping them back to his side, as well as several others, but it was concluded that he had drowned.

In an effort to get the little children away from their father, she had instructed them to go to the tent and pray. She said, "For 45 minutes those young children prayed for their dad."

Now, St. Anthony is located at least 45 miles south of where this accident happened, and 15 to 20 minutes passed from the time the father jumped into the water until the call was received by me. I'm sure that well over an hour had passed by the time we arrived at the accident scene. Jess and I were told that just 10 to 15 minutes before we came the victim began to breathe on his own and that he was somewhat stable, although not conscious.

By modern training standards, the resuscitation effort that was made by the people at that time was totally inadequate. However, there were some efforts made almost continuously to maintain his respiration.

We arrived at the Ashton hospital 25 minutes later, and the patient was checked by Dr. Krueger. Since he was beginning to regain consciousness, Dr. Krueger could see no reason for him to remain in the hospital. He recommended transporting him to Blackfoot where he lived.

We again loaded him into the ambulance. At St. Anthony, I let the sheriff out and picked up a new ambulance driver. By the time we arrived at the hospital in Blackfoot, the patient was alert and walked in unaided.

I have lost track of this special family. I don't even know their names, only that they are from Blackfoot and a rather young family.

I realize that the power of prayer was certainly instrumental in the process that occurred that Sunday afternoon, especially due to the faith and prayers of those little children. From a medical standpoint, I suspect that the victim always had a heartbeat and that there was just enough air exchange from the various methods of resuscitation that were attempted to properly oxygenate him.

It is my fervent testimony that a far greater power assisted in the healing process and that the miracle performed was due to the faith and prayers of that family. That is the real reason why this gentleman survived. It would be wonderful to know them again and to hear how they have fared the last twenty years.

Paul Romrell

FAITH—THE MIRACLE

The bishop had just stood up and announced to the congregation that we were to build a new meeting house. My husband and I looked at each other because we knew what this meant. We had been involved in many such projects in the past and knew that it would only be a short while before we were summoned to the bishop's office. Sure enough, our fears were realized and we found ourselves sitting directly across the desk from our bishop and his counselors. On the board behind them, printed in large letters, was the amount to be raised: $68,000.00. My husband and I had been very concerned as to how we would acquire the money necessary to pay our fair share.

We had received many blessings during our marriage, but being financially secure had not been one of them. Thus, before we went for our appointment with the bishop, we had called a family counsel. We discussed the problem with the children and received their full support in whatever figure we arrived at for our committment. Our oldest son, who was 12 at the time, had a paper route and told us that he would pay $60.00 from his paper route money. Our daughter who was nine had part of a paper route and pledged $20.00. That day we sat across from the bishop and knew we could pledge at least $80.00. How much my husband had decided to add to that amount I did not know. The bishop explained to us how much money was needed and then asked us to pledge what we thought was fair "and then some." This gave my husband the idea to tack on $100.00 to the $500.00 he had already decided to pledge. All I could think of during the rest of the interview with the bishopric was where in the world would we get $600.00?"

I later voiced this thought to my husband, who answered that he did not know but the Lord would provide. He always had, and he wouldn't let us down now especially when we were trying to do his will. The matter was dropped and we went on with our daily routine.

Christmas was quickly approaching. It had been two months since our meeting with the bishop. Our children had given us the $80.00 they had pledged, and we had been able to add almost two hundred dollars to that. We were still quite a bit short of our commitment.

On Saturday evening as we called our family together to begin our fast, we discussed with them the purposes for which we should fast. Our little Holly was quick to suggest that we should fast for money. We all got a chuckle out of that and then my husband replied, "Sister, we are not supposed to fast for money." She looked up at him with a hurt expression in her eyes, feeling badly that he had thought she had unrighteous motives and then said, "Not for us, but the building fund. We need to fast for money to pay the building fund." She was so sincere that we decided to include this in our prayers and we did. The next day was not only Fast Sunday but the first day of Hanukkah, a Jewish holiday celebrated around Christmastime each year. It is a festival of lights and lasts for eight days.

The reason our family is familiar with this holiday is that my husband, Ron, is a convert from Judaism and had celebrated this holiday many times as a child.

It was about 10:30 that night when the doorbell rang. When we got to the door, no one was there. There on the step was an envelope. Inside the envelope was a card that said Happy Hanukkah from Joseph to Judah. One large candle had been drawn on the card and inside were five, five-dollar bills. Needless to say, my husband and I were spellbound.

Who could have done this unselfish deed? The next morning as we explained to our children what had taken place the night before, my husband and I were still trying to guess who had left us this money. Our little girl looked up and with her pure childlike faith said, "We asked Heavenly Father for money and he gave it to us!" That ended our discussion as to where the money came from.

My husband and I knew that Hanukkah lasted for eight days but we didn't know if our Hanukkah visitor knew. We soon found out that he did because the second night of Hanukkah the bell rang again. We went to the door and discovered another card, this time with two candles. Along with the card was a metal box which contained thirteen two-dollar bills. We knew then that our Hanukkah visitor would come every night for eight nights.

The third night was twenty-five dollars in one-dollar bills. Then twenty-five dollars in half-dollars, then quarters, dimes, nickles, and on the last night of Hanukkah, there was a basket full of pennies and a one-hundred dollar bill on top. All together our Hanukkah visitor had brought us three hundred and one dollars, exactly half the amount we had pledged for the building fund.

There are other times when the faith of one is not sufficient and when our faith must be united with others to bring to pass a miracle. This was the circumstance that existed when our third child was born.

My husband and I were anxiously awaiting the arrival of our third child. I had just been wheeled into the delivery room and the long-awaited time was at hand. There were, however, more problems than we had anticipated. The baby's head had emerged and at that point, the birth process stopped. After much effort on the part of the doctor, he realized that the baby's shouders were too large to pass through the birth canal. He then made the decision to break the baby's collarbone in order that the baby could be born.

Shortly after birth our son took his first breath and then stopped breathing. On recognizing the problem, the doctor left me to help the baby. After working with him for what seemed like an eternity, but in actuality about five minutes, the baby took another breath. The thought kept going through my mind that there might be possible brain damage because oxygen had gone to the brain and then had been cut off for about five minutes.

I was taken to my room where I anxiously awaited the arrival of our son's pediatrician. When the pediatrician arrived, my first question was, "Does my son have brain damage?" The pediatrician responded that he didn't believe the baby did but they were running more tests to make sure. He told my husband and me there was no need to worry about the broken collarbone as baby's bones mend very rapidly. We would just have to handle him carefully for a while.

Then the doctor made a statement that is most dreaded by all parents. He said our baby's chance for survival was not very good. He went on to explain that in the course of examining the baby they discovered he had been born with a defective heart. The doctor explained that because of this defect the baby would probably have a heart attack within the next three days. He said that if the baby did live past the three days it would be necessary to perform open heart surgery.

The next few days seemed an eternity to us. Many of our friends and neighbors fasted and prayed for our son. This letter was read to my husband's seminary class two days after David was born.

Dear friends in my Daddy's Seminary class: As most of you know, I made my dramatic entry into this world Monday evening. All of my family was so happy I made it, especially Mommy. I've been waiting such a long time to come here to earth and now that I'm here, I'm looking forward to doing all the things there are to do in this earth life.

I want to go to seminary, like you guys, date, and go on a mission. I've wanted to be a missionary for Father ever since the Council in Heaven. I want to marry in the temple. With a mommy like I've got, I should be able to make it with no problem.

There is one problem though. The doctor told my parents I have something wrong with my heart, something about a part missing. He says the next three days will tell the difference. Either I'll make it, or I'll have a heart attack and die. I won't mind passing through the veil. After all, there is much for me to look forward to, but I would like to stay and enjoy this life.

My family have administered to me and some of them are fasting and praying for me. I sure would appreciate it if you would include me in your prayers—no telling how much it would help. Maybe I'll be able to do the same for you some day.

I've taken enough of your time; Daddy has a few things to teach you. Thanks friends, David Neal Zeidner

We notified my husband's family and explained the problem to them. My husband's sister was very concerned for the welfare of our child. She later explained to us that since she did not know how to pray she decided to call a church and ask them to pray for our baby. She couldn't remember the name of our church. All she could remember is that the name of Christ was part of the title. She looked in the phone directory and called all of the churches whose name had Christ included in them. She said she felt if she did this, she was sure to get the right one. She was not familiar with any of these churches because she is Jewish. She said she did feel that the faith and prayers of many Christians would benefit our baby.

Three days passed and all was well. We were allowed to take David home with us. He was an adorable baby. He was chubby and appeared to be very healthy. No one would have ever guessed the problems that were going on inside his little body. His arms had been taped to his body because of his broken collarbone and we had been instructed to be very careful when we handled him. Other than this, he appeared to be the picture of health.

The night before we were to take him back to the doctor, my husband and father administered to him. I was listening very carefully to the blessing. When I heard my husband pronounce that he would be healed immediately of all of his infirmities, I began to cry. After the blessing was over I asked my husband if he had been inspired to pronounce those words or if he wanted it so badly that he had thought it was inspiration. He told me that he had been inspired and the blessing had already come to pass. Our son had been healed. The next day we took him to the doctor. My husband told the doctor there was no need for an examination because our son had been healed. He went on to tell the doctor that if he really needed the fee he could go ahead and examine our son. The doctor looked at us with a twinkle in his eye letting us know he understood. You see, he was also a Melchizedeck Priesthood holder and realized that miracles happen.

The doctor examined our son and was delighted to inform us of something we already knew. Not only was the baby's heart in perfect condition, but he was unable to find any evidence of a broken collarbone. He told us to take our baby home and enjoy him. We did this with much eagerness and gratitude in our hearts.

Two weeks after David was born we received this letter from a Church of Christ minister in Willingsboro, New Jersey, where my sister-in-law lives:

Dear David, I just finished talking with Mrs. Rimorin, a relative of yours, whom you haven't met yet. She tells me you are doing jsut fine now—eating like a pig and growing. By the time you're old enough to read this letter, the difficult times your parents faced at your birth will have long since been made light of. Praise the Lord! The prayers of a lot of fine people for your welfare have been answered. Truly the Lord moves in mysterious ways. Perhaps your parents will save this letter so that you will know that your birth was something special, not only to them but to others also.

David, study your Bible, for it is God's word given to man. It holds the knowledge of eternal life. It can be yours only if you study and obey its commands. Our Lord and Savior Jesus Christ, died on Calvary's cross, not only for your sins, but for the sins of the whole world so that you might spend eternity with him. Believe Him! May you always remain as innocent as you are now. May the

*Lord bless you as you grow. May you always bring joy
and happiness wherever you go. Love has conceived you
and breathed the breath of life into you. Don't ever forget
it! Rejoice in the Lord always. Your brother in Christ,
Roger Chain.*

Our family was very touched by the love and faith
that spanned the miles to reach our home during our
time of need. We have been ever grateful for this
experience and have been greatly strengthened in the
power of faith and prayer.

This experience is still touching the lives of
others. We just recently received a letter from an elder in
the field—thanking my husband for the things he had
been taught in seminary and expressing gratitude for
being allowed to share in this experience concerning
David. It was this experience that increased his faith
sufficiently to create within him a desire to go on a
mission.

Faith is needed today as much as ever. Little can
we see. We do not know what tomorrow will bring.
Accidents, sickness, even death, seem to hover over us
continually. Little do we know when they might strike.

It takes faith to follow the living prophet, to plant
a garden, to obtain a year's supply of food, go on a
mission, to pay tithes when funds are scarce and
demands are great, to pledge money that you do not
have to the building fund. It takes faith to fast and have
family prayers. It takes faith to withstand adversity and
emerge a better person rather than a bitter one.

Just as faith in ancient times has made firey flames
ineffective, opened dry corridors through rivers and seas,
and manifested many other miracles, so in our day, faith
can heal the sick, bring comfort to those who mourn,

strengthen resolve against tempation, and lead to a sure knowledge of the divinity of Jesus Christ.

Exercise the faith and the miracle will come.

Janie Zeidner

"TRUST IN THE LORD WITH ALL THINE HEART"

Ethel Verna Hackworth was a small, attractive young woman, weighing less than a hundred pounds, but she had plenty of spunk.

Like her faithful convert parents, Edgar and Nannie Tuck Hackworth, she developed an abiding testimony of the truthfulness of the restored gospel of Jesus Christ. This precious testimony became an integral part of her, an anchor, a constant source of strength and guidance.

She was born November 22, 1901, in Old Virginia, as she lovingly called Dundee, Bedford County. At age 12, she came by train in 1914 with her parents, four sisters, and two brothers, ages 11 to 1, settling in Teton, Idaho. Later her folks homesteaded on an old sand ranch located north of Big Grassy Ridge, five miles north of Parker, Idaho. Their nearest neighbors were Roy and Leonard Jenkins. Beyond them a few miles lived her mother's brothers, Ed and Eldridge Tuck, and Eldridge's wife, Rosella.

Ethel soon learned that life out West was tough. She and her beloved brother, Allie, age 14, were best friends. On a beautiful Sunday afternoon August 12, 1917, Ethel and her little sister Grace, age 8, were playing paper dolls. Allie kept teasing them by opening the door and letting the wind blow the dolls off the table. Ethel sputtered saying, "Get out of here and stop being such a tease."

Later, Allie, Grace and their brother Chick, age 6, were outside riding stick horses. Allie said, "Let's go to the sands. Mother won't care if we go this one time." So off they went on their stick horses.

Allie decided to dig a cave. He would crawl back in the hole and the other two youngsters would take hold of his legs and pull him out with an armful of sand. Then they heard a strange noise and noticed the sand had caved in on him, only his legs were protruding. Their faithful dog tried to dig him out and so did they, but the sand kept falling down. (The muffled sound was Allie trying to call them.)

Realizing they needed help, they ran home to get their mother and Ethel. Their dad and Iva, age 12, had gone to Teton. Grace stayed at home with Ora, Chick, Helen, and Hubert.

Ethel and her mother grabbed shovels and hurried, hoping to rescue Allie. They frantically dug him from the sand, praying as they worked. They dislodged sand from his throat and attempted to revive him, but it was too late—Allie was gone.

Ethel remained with Allie while their mother trudged five miles through the sand to obtain help. She couldn't find a soul at the Jenkins' place so she rushed on to tell her brothers the sad news. Grace put a lamp in the window so those who searched for Allie could locate their home in the pitch-dark night. The coyotes were howling and Ethel was alone in that sandbowl with Allie's head on her lap.

The men came on horses and brought Chick to assist them in finding Ethel and Allie. After hollering "E-T-H-E-L" several times, she answered and they finally located them. They brought Allie in on horseback. (Grace later said, "To this day when I am watching a western movie and see someone being brought in over a horse, I always turn my head." Then she mentioned, "I remember that after Allie's untimely death, a buggy ran over Hubert's stomach when someone was turning around with those darn horses. Mother said, 'This farm is sure mean to my boys.' ")

Time passed, Ethel grew up and fell in love. She and William Walter Burt, a typical, cowboy-type westerner, were married June 5, 1920. Ethel and others called him Will, but most of his friends called him Bill. They knew happiness was in store for them.

By 1926, four children were adding joy to their lives: Gene, Cyril, Betty, and Charles Edgar, who was born June 26th that year at Fruitvale, Idaho. Charles Edgar lived only a few hours. This was one of many sad events that would test their faith and hearts.

A third son, David Estel, arrived August 29, 1927. They called him their "derrick boy." The Burt family would one day own a farm. Dad would be the haystacker, Gene and Cyril would drive the horses on the hay wagon, and of course, David would drive the derrick horse. Surely there couldn't be a happier family.

That winter the temperatures ranged from 20 to 30 degrees below zero. Ethel and Will lived on the Grant Packer place just below the old steel bridge in Twin Groves, Fremont County, Idaho. They worked for him, milking 22 head of cows by hand. Their house stood near the head of the St. Anthony Canal by the dam called the Big V. Will's job provided them with a little extra money, so they purchased a fairly good supply of groceries for the winter, including 100 pounds of flour and some potatoes. Bill butchered a big hog to provide them with some roasts, tasty pork chops, etc.

This young couple often talked about their many blessings, such as: four children, relatives, the Church, friends, a warm home, a job, and plenty to eat. All they actually needed was more wood. But their dreams didn't materialize as planned. The mortgage company came and took the cows, thus Will's job abruptly ended. Grant said they could live in the house until spring.

Christmas was only two weeks away. It was bitter cold with plenty of snow for Santa Claus' sleigh. Will and his brother, Harry, of Chester, and Ray Hope (Harry's son-in-law) decided to go to Warm River with teams and sleighs and haul wood that Harry had banked near Big Falls (now known as Upper Mesa Falls). They planned to haul it to Warm River and then home. It was 22 miles from the Packer place to Warm River and another 7 miles farther to Big Falls. Grant loaned Will a team of black mares. They loaded the sleighs with hay for the horses, grub for the men, and headed for the mountains.

They stayed in a sheep camp (a canvas covered wagon with a small stove in it) at Warm River. The wagon was used for cooking and sleeping. This was quite a project due to the snow and cold weather. Perhaps swinging that old cross-cut saw by hand and the double-bitted axe kept them in such good physical condition that they could have endured most anything.

While the fellows were getting out wood at Warm River, Ethel was home caring for their four small children. The little derrick boy was now four months old. This was a tremendous responsibility for her to assume without her companion's help. During those bitter, cold winter days she must have often reflected upon her earlier life in Lynchburg, Virginia.

It was the 20th of December. The weather was cold and clear, and old Snake River was frozen solid with snow and ice. Cecil Allen, a neighbor and good friend, had traded Will out of an old, Oakland car and had decided to bring his team of horses and pull the car home. The weather had warmed up considerably; it was a gorgeous day.

As he and Ethel visited in the yard, Cecil happened to look up the river. He exclaimed, "Ethel, the river is starting to flood over its bank. You better get the kids and run for safety." He turned his horses loose, grabbed Gene and Betty and headed for the road to higher ground. In the meantime, Ethel ran into the house for her baby, took Cyril by the hand and followed Cecil Allen's example of heading for the road. But it was too late!

The rushing flood of water with its snow and ice looked like a large herd of huge sheep. As Ethel and her two little boys reached the lowland, the gorge-ice and rushing water bowled them over like tenpins in a bowling alley. She managed to get back on her feet, but couldn't swim a stroke. She thought she still had David in her arms, but all she had was his frozen blanket. Her little derrick boy was gone. Ethel was sure she had lost Cyril but felt certain she still had David.

About the time she realized David was missing, she saw Cyril caught between two chunks of ice with his legs bent back like he was kneeling with a big chunk of ice pinning him there. He was about a rod away from her and floating with the gorge-ice. As the rushing water forced the ice jam to the side, it caused the ice to start building up and stopping. Ethel began working her way to Cyril through waist-deep water, but when she got to him it was impossible to free him. She kept pawing the slush ice and water that built up around him, and she worked his arms up and down to keep him from freezing. She worked frantically to keep his head above the water. This probably saved her own life as well as that of her four-year-old son.

The huge body of water had floated them about 200 yards from where they were when the water first hit them. Ethel had struggled for their lives, swimming and climbing over gorge-ice until the ice jammed against the levee that went through the field. The levee stopped the ice that had Cyril trapped.

Will was now approaching the steel bridge that crossed the Snake River. His sleigh was slipping easily along the snow covered road, the wood well loaded on the bunks of the sleigh. There was a Christmas tree on top, and he was thinking how good it would be to arrive home and how much fun Christmas would be. He visualized a cheery fire and all the wonderful things this special holiday brings.

Suddenly, he heard a roaring, ripping sound as the ice broke in the river. The warming weather had caused the water and ice that had backed up the river for miles to break and start flowing. Will's account of this experience follows:

"While traveling along, all at once I heard the most alarming noise. I saw and heard ice breaking in the river and watched water pushing ice onto the banks. When I reached Flo Maines' place, I saw him run and jerk his corral gates open and all the sheep run up toward the road. The ice was to his corral, in fact, right up to his barn.

"I traveled on, thinking that is the worst gorge I've ever seen! The river was rising and I could see across it to Mr. Ellingson's place. It was throwing the snow and ice across the road that goes past his house, and even on the land I'd been farming. I hadn't thought about our house being in danger. It seemed to me the water was going down the river.

I drove the meadow along the river, ice was going out on the road in front of me. I went through it and on up the hill to the bridge. It was then I noticed ice going towards MY house! Cecil Allen was turning his team loose. I couldn't cross the bridge with the load of logs, so I tied the team to the fence and ran across it. The bridge was yanking and jerking, and the water was over my shoe tops.

A sleigh came along and I jumped on hoping to soon reach my place. Neighbors were gathering there, but it was impossible for anyone to cross the rushing water to aid Ethel who was standing waist-deep in icy water. Being unaware of Cyril's critical predicament, people could not figure out why Ethel didn't go to higher ground.

I jumped from the sleigh and started to run across the water. Some men grabbed me and threw me into a sleigh box. They knew I couldn't make it across the raging water. They attempted going around the body of water that was building up to the west. Six of us men jumped into the sleigh. They ran the team down around the water. When they came up along the canal bank and got as close to Ethel as they could, I hopped out and tried to reach her. I couldn't make it straight across the water, so I ran up stream, got in and worked my way to her and Cyril. Water was running on both sides of the canal.

Suddenly, a large piece of ice jammed up in the water between Ethel, Cyril, the team and sleigh, and myself. Fortunately, ice built up forming a bridge. Clarence Liesburg quickly slid across the ice bridge, grabbed Ethel by the hand and helped her to the sleigh. I lifted the ice off Cyril's legs and carried him across the ice bridge to his shocked and terrified, but relieved, mother.

The men had to hurry to get the team and sleigh back to the road before the water and ice became too deep. As they drove the team across the water and ice the water ran over the top of the sleigh box, and the team was forced to swim. The weight of the men in the sleigh and their quick actions held the box in the bunks of the bobsleigh as the well-trained team lunged across the ice and water. Thanks be to God for brave men and smart horses!"

According to Florence Packer (Grant's wife), who lived up the hill from Will and Ethel's, the dear soul was in the water for at least 30 minutes. She said they took Ethel and Cyril to Mr. Ellingson's place northeast of the old steel bridge. They wrapped them in warm blankets and rubbed life into their frozen bodies. (For the next 61 years Florence and Cyril have been great friends. She still calls him her "miracle boy.")

Christmas that year was not as merry for Will and Ethel as they'd anticipated. Their little derrick boy was buried somewhere beneath all that gorge-ice and snow along the banks of the Snake River. Will spent countless hours and days walking over the ice pack that winter, searching in vain for his little son.

Ethel Verna Hackworth Burt—MY MOTHER— the kindest, bravest and loveliest person in the world, whose destiny it was to know many tragedies, hardships, and sorrow during her lifetime, said this to us children many times: "Trust in the Lord with all thine heart; and lean not unto thine own understanding.

In all thy ways acknowledge him and he shall direct thy paths" (Proverbs 3:5-6).

I testify that she loved the Lord and trusted him and that he protected and directed her. It is my constant prayer that some day I can do something to partially repay this lovely lady for what she did for me on that eventful day in December, 1927, as well as for the many,

many things she has done since then for me—and not only for me, but for my wife, Maxine, and our family.

Cyril O. Burt

HIS LOVING CARE

In February 1944, my huband, Marvin, our baby Sheila, and I were living in a government housing project called University of Homes in Portland, Oregon. Marvin was employed as a rigger in the Kaiser shipyards.

On February 29, my uncle Adrian Carter died. He was from our hometown of St. Anthony. He lived near us and worked in the shipyards. I accompanied his wife, Ivy, and their family to Idaho for his funeral.

We planned to attend the Twin Groves Ward reunion on March 17 and start for home the next day. On the 13th, my two older brothers and Marvin's younger brother were called to Pocatello for induction into the navy. Both our families were upset.

That day, Uncle Ralph Carter, also of Portland, came to dinner at my parents' home. He said he'd seen Marvin climbing around in the rigging of the ships for the last month. This was horrifying news. Three months before, because of a doctor's work order, Marvin had been moved from rigging to work on the ways and that's exactly what I thought he had been doing. I started to tremble and to have such a hollow feeling.

That night I had a vivid and very disturbing dream. I dreamed I was in our apartment. A man came to the door. Instantly, his coal-black and dark, piercing eyes caught my attention. He wore black, horn-rimmed glasses. He said, "I'm the trouble-shooter from the shipyards where your husband works. He has been accidentally injured and is in the hospital in critical condition."

The next morning I told Mother, "If I believed in dreams, I would leave for home immediately." Then I related my dream. She attempted to calm me saying that I was probably upset over my brothers leaving for the navy and also due to Ralph's report about Marvin.

The remaining time passed surprisingly fast. We had family pictures taken and enjoyed family gatherings with the boys.

On the 18th, we went to Pocatello to catch the Portland Rose train. As often happened in those days, we had a flat tire. The train left without us and we spent a long, tedious night in the depot. Towards evening the stationmaster said the Streamliner would be there in an hour and that someone had cancelled their reservation. He suggested that I take the available seat and get my baby home. I arrived in Portland at eight o'clock the next morning, in about half the time it would have taken me on the train.

My neighbor and friend, Rosie, was shocked to learn that I hadn't heard about Marvin's accident. She related, "On the morning of the 13th, your husband fell from an unbelievable height, sixty feet at least, and landed on a steel deck. He slipped on the frost-covered ladder he was using. It's the biggest wonder in the world he's still alive." After telling me the extent of his injuries, she talked about the terrible thoughts she'd been having because she felt I had purposely stayed away.

I later learned that Marvin's feet were so terribly broken that the doctors wanted to amputate them, but they had to have my permission. Marvin feared they might scare me into consenting to the operation so he told them he had contacted me, but that I couldn't come.

I hurried by taxi to see him. Upon entering the hospital room, I saw a man in bed, but I was certain someone had made a mistake. This person looked ten years older than my husband. But it *was* Marvin. Both his feet were in casts up to his knees; he was in a body cast, too, because his back had been broken in two places. He told me that his casts had been put on that morning. His doctor explained that there was no way they could have set the shattered bones in his feet and ankles so they just pushed them into the shape of feet and casted them.

After Marvin and I had talked for 15 minutes, a man walked in. I knew at a glance I'd seen him before. Of course, *he* was the man in my dream! His name was John Apts, the "trouble-shooter" who would have brought me the news of Marvin's accident.

Ironically, this man later talked me into going to the shipyard to turn in Marvin's badge and hard hat to sign him out. He said it was necessary procedure for me to get his paycheck. Afterwards, we learned that if I hadn't signed him out, we could have sued and most assuredly won the case as the company had ignored the doctor's work order and put him back in rigging.

Marvin's bone specialist told me that he would never be able to walk without crutches and possibly not even with them. Back in 1940, Marvin had shot the big toe off his right foot in a hunting accident. This greatly added to his present problem.

Two days later when I visited Marvin, his doctor told me, "Because your husband is in such terrific pain, we are unable to find a pain killer that will allow him to sleep. It's vital that he does because the human body can only go so long without sleep, then something 'snaps'—probably his mind."

Marvin looked worse each day. His eyes were glassy, and his pupils had dilated due to the drugs he'd been given. The doctor asked my permission to give him stronger doses of morphine, then added, "I can't promise it will help."

Our mothers came to be with us. The first thing they asked was, "Have the elders administered to Marvin?" I had the mistaken idea that one called them *only* when a person was dying.

The bishop of our small ward, Bishop George, brought Elder Tolman, and we all went together to the hospital. I hadn't mentioned to anyone what the doctor had said about Marvin's not ever being able to walk. I couldn't put that into words. When Bishop George asked what he should pray for, I replied, "Please ask that the doctor can find *some* way to help Marvin sleep."

Bishop George gave him a remarkable, comforting blessing. He asked our Heavenly Father to bless him that he would be able to sleep and, in addition, that he would be able to walk and to rear a family.

Following the blessing, the bishop talked to Marvin. Elder Tolman called me aside and said, "Now, don't you worry about your husband being able to walk because if he weren't going to, Bishop George would not have pronounced those particular words in his behalf." And I never worried again about this grave concern.

Before we left the hospital that day, the doctor called me into his ofice and said they had found a new drug that they had been using for the men in military hospitals, but it was necessary that I give my permission for Marvin to use it.

The next day when I visited him, he was asleep! What an exciting moment that was. He only slept for two hours, but it was a beginning. But because they wouldn't let him remain in a private room and because he couldn't sleep where there were any distractions, the doctor said it was OK to take him home.

It was a difficult struggle, yet we were overwhelmed by the kindnesses and compassion shown by his fellow shipyard workers. The day after I signed him out, they gave us over $800 which they had collected. This was followed by another collection enabling them to buy him a wheelchair. Some of the workers constantly dropped in to visit and to bring thoughtful gifts. One special, elderly fellow brought bags of black walnuts. Marvin would shell them, then I'd take them to a candy kitchen to be sold for $2 a pound.

When the doctor took Marvin's last cast off about eight months later, he asked, "How soon may I try to walk?" The doctor gave me such a disgusted look and said, "Any damn time you feel like you can."

On our way home we stopped at the labor office for crutches. No sooner were we in our apartment than Marven tried to stand. And he did stand until his perspiring face turned a sickly green. That was another encouraging step.

We kept our faith, and I rubbed oil on his feet and ankles, then put heavy wool socks on him. We didn't have a tub so I attached a canvas hose to the showerhead and Marvin would sit in the shower letting hot water run over his feet for hours at a time. We continually thanked Heavenly Father for his many blessings, and we humbly let him know that we needed his help.

Within six weeks when Marvin walked into the doctor's office with the help of his canes, the doctor nearly fainted. He called his assistant to note Marvin's amazing progress. The assistant exclaimed, "I don't believe in man, God, or in the devil, but I didn't have anything to do with that!"

In February, 1945, I went to a different doctor as I was expecting a new baby. He showed me a medical journal in which Marvin's case was recorded. It showed pictures of his X-rays and gave other interesting details. It stated that because the state of Oregon wouldn't pay for Marvin to have further surgery, he would walk in pain the rest of his life.

That same month the doctors released Marvin and we returned to St. Anthony to live. In May, Janine was born, and within three years, Becky arrived; nine years later, Laurie completed our family. These girls have been a constant joy to us. I question if anyone could have had a finer example of faith, courage, and ambition than their dad has been to them—and to me.

In 1980 when Laurie married Val Corier of Seattle, we learned that his favorite uncle was none other than Judson Tolman, our friend who had assisted in administering to Marvin forty years previously.

When the doctors released Marvin, he was given total disability by the state. He understood that he could do anything to supplement his income. His monthly check of $62 was gradually increased over the years.

In 1981, while working for the U.S. Post office as a rural mail carrier, the state of Oregon informed Marvin that he must go to their doctor in Portland. The doctor turned out to be the assistant doctor Marvin first had on his case. He insisted Marvin wasn't that badly disabled. We felt he either didn't understand the true facts, or he was heartless. At that time, Marvin's feet and ankles had deteriorated to the point that he was experiencing more pain than he'd had since being back on his feet. As a result of that doctor's erroneous report, the State gave

Marvin only a small settlement and cancelled his compensation.

On December 13, 1984, Marvin fell off our garage, shattering his left hip and elbow. Again it was due to our faith in the Lord Jesus Christ and in his priesthood power that Marvin was able to face further pain, casts, and bone grafts.

When he fell in the shipyards, it was, indeed, a miracle that he wasn't killed. Another man fell 10 feet and was killed. We reaffirm that if it had not been for the power and gifts of the priesthood and Heavenly Father's loving care, Marvin would be spending his life in a wheelchair.

Hilda Carter Waldram

Part Two

TESTIMONIES

of

CONVERTS

"Now therefore ye are no more strangers and foreigners, but fellow citizens with the saints, and of the household of God;

And are built upon the foundation of the apostles and prophets, Jesus Christ himself being the chief corner stone."

—Ephesians 2:19,20.

LET'S BE MORMONS

Our conversion to Mormonism may amuse some, but to my wife, Sandy, and me, it was, and continues to be the greatest blessing we have experienced.

I was reared as Pentacostal Holiness and Sandy as a Baptist. When we married in 1975, neither of us wanted to convert to the other's religion. Consequently, we deprived ourselves of many spiritual blessings since we did not attend church.

Finally after nine years of marital happiness except for feeling "something" was lacking, we decided it was time to find a church that would meet our needs. We really wanted God in our lives, and we felt it was important now for our sons, Brian, eight, and Shaun, seven, to know more than they did about the Savior and his teachings. We were puzzled. "What church should we join?" was our constant query.

One day I said jokingly to Sandy, "Let's be Mormons." Her reply astonished me, "OK" Although we both appeared to be jesting, inside we were very serious. We thought we should also consider investigating Catholic beliefs.

Not long afterwards, I attended a baseball game of one of our boys. You guessed it. I met a Mormon, Norma Anderson. Sandy called her on the phone that night and asked her where we could locate a Mormon church.

They talked for some length, and Sister Anderson invited us to dinner a week later, adding she would have the sisters over that night to meet us.

We expected the sisters to be two old spinsters. I wish you could have seen the expressions on our faces when we met two young girls instead. After dinner, they presented the first missionary discussion about the Godhead. We heard glorious principles and doctrine that were completely new to both of us, but which we felt were of utmost importance. They explained that the elders should teach us since we lived in their area, but they would check on it.

Sandy and I later discussed this and decided we didn't want two old men to teach us. We preferred these young women. They didn't realize that we understood the word *elder* to mean "old." Sister Dart, of Salem, Utah, and Sister Murawski, of Akron, Ohio, received permission to teach us. Sandy and I knew after the second discussion on the plan of life that we would become Mormons. We learned about pre-earth life, the importance and purpose of mortality, and life after death.

The missionaries commented that we should have been members all along for we readily accepted their gospel teachings and hungered after each discussion to learn more. They encouraged us to pray and to read and study the scriptures. Our prayers were answered almost immediately. It was gratifying to realize that in our pre-earth life we developed talents; that death is not the end of life, and that we can live together as families eternally through obedience to God's commandments, ordinances, and covenants.

When the Word of Wisdom was taught to us, Sandy and I agreed to quit smoking cigarettes and to live this law. The sisters asked if we would like to have Elder

Aune, of Park City, Utah, and Elder Morgan, of Manchester, Missouri, give each of us a priesthood blessing so we would have added strength to succeed in our resolve. Their concern impressed us, and we thought this would be a special privilege.

I told Sandy, "I guess we'll meet these two old men." We were as shocked at seeing the two young elders as we had been when we first met the sister missionaries.

We encountered no problems in observing the Word of Wisdom. In fact, I felt I didn't need the blessing to achieve my goal but never told anyone, not even Sandy. After my blessing, Elder Morgan looked at me and commented, "Brother Shirley, you didn't need the blessing, did you?" I acknowledged his perceptive observation.

In addition to praying and studying as counseled by the missionaries, my wife and I compared and evaluated our former beliefs with those taught by these fine missionaries. During the remaining discussions, we had the opportunity of being taught by both the sisters and the two elders. They were interested in hearing what we had formerly believed.

Members of the Holiness Church don't believe in smoking or drinking alcoholic beverages, and they avoid caffeine. Sandy's former Baptist Church allowed people to smoke outside on the grounds but not inside. Even the minister smoked.

In the Holiness Church, women are encouraged not to wear makeup or a lot of jewelry. They have a very plain look. There are a few programs offered young people, but a youth service is usually held each Sunday night prior to the regular Sunday evening service. Members are admonished to observe the law of tithing, but its purpose is not fully explained. I always knew I should pay ten percent of my earnings for tithing, but I didn't know why. An auxiliary meeting is held once a month for women. It's not as comprehensive a program as Relief Society in the LDS Church. They have lots of music in the Holiness Church. It has a beat to it, "foot-stomping, soul-moving music." They usually have a guitar and a piano. They believe in speaking in tongues and call this being filled with the Holy Ghost.

I have never been in a Holiness Church where every member believed the same way. On the contrary, I found it assuring that the LDS Church is so well organized and directed that members are taught and exhorted to live the same principles and doctrine throughout the world in every ward and stake. And the sincere feeling of love and friendship exhibited wherever one attends is also noteworthy. The members have more opportunities for growth and to use their talents than in many other churches because they conduct the various meetings, teach the classes, and deliver the talks and musical numbers, which involves members of all ages.

Sandy and I were baptized May 27, 1984, by Brother Ray Anderson and confirmed by Elder Aune, assisted by Elder Morgan. I had the privilege of baptizing Brian when he was eight; he was confirmed by Elder Morgan.

It has been a highlight to us, as well as a good influence on our sons, to wlecome the lady missionaries and the elders in our home. They know our home is thiers, a home away from home where they can relax on their preparation day, eat with us, stop for some cold water, or just talk. One, among many, who has become very dear to us, is Elder Monte Webster, of Idaho Falls, Idaho. Brian and Shaun consistently save their money and plan to serve the Lord on missions as the young people they have met and love are doing.

Sandy and I are humbly grateful for some specific evidences that, to our knowledge, are only found in the LDS Church:

A personal visitation of God the Father and his Son, Jesus Christ, after centuries of spiritual darkness to the Prophet Joseph Smith to reveal the true personality of the Godhead and to open the door to the establishment of the dispensation of the fulness of times.

The coming of the Angel Moroni, a resurrected being, with the plates from which the book of Mormon was translated and published in 1830, another testament of Jesus Christ.

The coming of John the Baptist with the Aaronic Priesthood, the power to baptize by immersion for the remission of sins.

The coming of Peter, James, and John with the holy Melchizedek Priesthood and the apostleship, the power to organize the church and kingdom of God in the earth for the last time to prepare the way for the second coming of the Savior of the world.

The authority to administer ordinances to individuals that through their qualifications and obedience will save and exalt them.

We feel certain that the day we said, "Let's be Mormons" was the greatest day of our lives.

David L. Shirley

THE CELESTIAL KINGDOM, PLEASE

I was born in Reno, Nevada in 1950. I came from a good family, but religion wasn't high priority. Dad worked hard, so we spent our weekends hunting, fishing, and boating. As a child, I went to church mainly on special occasions, like Easter and at Christmas. I had very little knowledge about any church.

Sharing the details leading to my conversion is exciting to me and strengthens my testimony. When I was twenty, I moved to Ogden, Utah, where I taught at the Allied Health School at Weber State College and worked for one of the Church hospitals. As I had prepared to leave Nevada, some of my friends warned, "Boy, you are in deep trouble. If you go to Utah, the Mormons will get you." I replied, "Mormons? What's a Mormon?" Their smart reply was, "Don't worry, Skip, you'll find out."

In Utah, I found Mormons everywhere. Some of them were poor examples of their religion, other exceptional. After a few encounters with LDS missionaries and seeing more Church members' bad examples, I became convinced that the Mormons would not "get" me. I concluded, "After all, who needs religion anyway, especially one that isn't important enough for its members to live its teachings?"

I became very critical of Mormons. I judged the Church by the people I knew instead of judging the Church by its unique teachings. I loved to poke fun at Mormons.

As I continued meeting Mormons, I was impressed by many good people. Somehow I had not associated their "goodness" with their religion. Before long, one of these Mormon girls, Deanna Fail, became my sweetheart and wife. We were married in September, 1973.

My thinking about Mormons began to change. My parents had just two children, my brother and myself, so I wasn't used to large families. Deanna invited me to dinner at her home one weekend to get acquainted with her parents. I'll never forget that experience. I immediately noticed the confusion and commotion. The television was loud; somebody was playing the piano, someone else a guitar. Meanwhile, Deanna's mother was trying her best to get everyone to the table. I thought, "How do these people live like this?"

As I watched the noisy children gather for prayer at dinnertime, it became evident that this family had a special spirit and close bond I had not found in my life. They had a calmness, peace, and security that was new to me. I couldn't put my finger on it, but I knew this family was different from mine, and I admired them.

As I continued to date Deanna, to be in her home and around her family, I was amazed that not one of them criticized my actions. They accepted me for the person I was. They didn't say, "Why don't you go to church on weekends?" Their considerate manner was important to me and stayed in my mind. I now know, whereas I didn't then, that our Heavenly Father works in mysterious ways. He gets things done in his own way through people he selects.

Being caught up in the things of the world, however, I didn't think I could give them up for religion. After all, why would I want to belong to a church that told me what I must do on weekends, how much money to donate for tithing, how to dress, what not to eat or drink, and even where and how to be married. That sounded dictatorial to me.

As time passed, I learned many things, one of which was flying planes. This became an obsession. Soon I became a flight instructor. I became really interested in these Mormons when I worked with Tom Humphrey, a special person who lived his religion. He tried in many ways to give me this gift which he valued so much. He loved the Lord and his church above all else and was not afraid to let others know his feelings. He never made a decision without consulting the Lord. He truly lived God's commandments. Often while we worked under an airplane, he would tell me about the gospel. He invited me to his home to teach me, but I wasn't cooperative. Nonetheless, he planted seeds and made a quiet, indelible impression on me.

In April, 1980, Deanna and I moved to Spring Glen, Utah, where we met another group of Mormons. Among them were doctors and their families. They, too, loved their religion and lived it. And they, too, tried to give me this gift that was so priceless to them.

We went on get-away flying trips together and learned to fly cross-country. I now know they were fellowshipping trips. At the time, I thought Deanna and I were helping them. The gospel was becoming more familiar, yet not visibly affecting me, I thought. I still wasn't ready to give up my freedom. I did not realize that these people (Jim and Sherleen Jaussi, Ted and Sharon Madsen, and others), were praying for me to recognize the light of the gospel and join their church. I was teaching several of them to fly. These friends' comments impressed me more later than they did at the time. For example, after a meeting we attended with them in Las Vegas, Nevada, Sherleen said, "You know, Craig, you would be a good Mormon if you didn't drink coffee." After that same meeting, we went to a show in one of the casinos and were entertained by Bill Cosby. Most of his jokes were related to families. Several with large families were present, and we enjoyed the show immensely. Later Jim commented, "I would have loved that show tonight because he is the funniest guy I've ever seen, but he didn't have to use the Lord's name in vain." Comments like that stayed with me.

Then came the ultimate experience that will affect our family forever.

At 6:00 a.m on a clear Tuesday, June 23, 1981, I sent Sherleen Jaussi, a petite mother of five, out into the blue yonder for her solo flight.

Sherleen was an exacting person and an excellent pilot. I felt she was better trained in emergency procedures than most student pilots.

At noon, Jim, her husband, appeared with a worried look and said she had not returned. Being an optimist, I was sure she was just late. By 6:00 p.m. we had to face the reality of her spending the night in the trees, or worse. I was saddened and felt great responsibility.

Difficult days followed. I could find no comfort. Surprisingly, no matter how long and disheartening the days became, Jim became stronger. We knew he was trying not to eat and drinking little water in order to feel Sherleen's condition.

He was concerned about my feelings. He never once censured me for insisting that Sherleen make her solo flight. He said, "I have no regrets or ill feelings toward you. When Sherleen and I made the decision to learn to fly, we made it a matter of prayer. If it is our Heavenly Father's will for her to die, I will accept it and rear our children in the Church."

Being a nonreligious person, I was surprised to see a man with such total trust and faith in an unseen being. I was touched by his calmness and strength. Now I know Jim was directed and comforted through this experience by the Holy Ghost.

Another marvelous example of the influence of the Holy Ghost concerns Ted and Sharon Madsen. They commenced each day with prayer and new hope that Sherleen would be located. They and other ward members never gave up the idea of making a ground search. They knew that if they did, through faith and the Lord's blessings, they would find her.

After Sherleen was found on Saturday morning by three excited men, she was taken to St. Mary's Hospital at Grand Junction. As Deanna and I were driving there, I tried to prepare her. I said, "Remember she hasn't eaten for nearly five days or had anything to drink; she's been in an aircraft accident and and will look really bad, so don't you go 'Ohhhhh!'" Later when we arrived, Deanna exclaimed, "She looks just like she did the morning she left on her solo flight." We both marveled at how well she had been protected and preserved. Then Sherleen said, "Craig, I'm so sorry about your airplane."

In retrospect, Deanna and I feel humbly grateful that we had the choice privilege to be in the pilots' lounge that Saturday morning with the men who had volunteered to perform the ground search, men from Sherleen's and Jim's ward who held the Melchizedek Priesthood. Everyone was reverent. It was inspiring. It would have been easy to hear a pin drop during Jim and Ted's talks and the special prayer petitioning Heavenly

Father's guidance and help. Only Deanna and I remained after the ground searchers cleared the room.

During the days I assisted Jim and others in attempts to find Sherleen, I now recognize and appreciate the many blessings that were evident. I also cannot deny that it was through the power and blessings of the priesthood that she was found. It wasn't just a coincidence. These people had something I didn't. I made a decision at that point in time that I wanted that "something."

I requested that some of the Seventies teach me the gospel and answer my questions. Their discussions were enlightening and impressive. They explained that each of us learns the gospel step by step and that nobody starts at the top.

Then I had what I considered a profound thought. I was overwhelmed that it had not entered my mind before. I reasoned, "When a person goes to college for a particular degree, he talks to his counselor about the requirements. The counselor explains which classes to take. He outlines the steps necessary to achieve certain goals.

"This is similar to the Lord's plan of life and exaltation. There is a way to reach the highest degree in the celestial kingdom, but in order to attain this goal we must proceed one step at a time. We aren't allowed to start at the top."

Once I realized that and made that analogy, it was easy for me to decide to join the Church. I told the Seventies and Deanna I wanted to be baptized. She was so shocked and elated that she almost fell off her chair!

I knew the Lord guided those men involved in the ground search as surely as if he had taken their hand and led them to Sherleen. I could not deny this evidence. When the news media asked, "How did you find her?"

Gardell Grundvig, one of the search party, responded, "Well, we know how we found her, but it's hard to explain." That's the way it was with me—hard to explain.

Deanna and I have found many miracles centered in the big one, but the greatest miracle of all is the unconditional love our Savior has for each of us. I know he will go to great lengths to rescue a soul if we ask, listen, and live his teachings. I feel, as did my student pilot, that the Lord did not want her found until he was ready for her to be found. I am grateful that she was found, and I'm grateful as well that I was found. I love the gospel and appreciate the prayers and interest of all who helped me gain a testimony. I will never be able to thank Jim and Sherleen, Ted and Sharon, Tom and others sufficiently for their genuine concern and exemplary lives.

In time I realize I didn't have to give up anything. Three months from the day Sherleen was found I was baptized by Deanna's father, Vaughn Fail, and confirmed by Brother James Jaussi. I accepted this precious gift with all my heart, and my gratitude for it increases as time goes on. Deanna and I became actively (and happily) involved in the Church.

I hope our family attains that highest degree in the Celestial kingdom as we work and serve faithfully throughout our lives and emulate the high ideals of others. I know the Savior lives, that our Heavenly Father hears and answers prayer, and that they love us unconditionally.

Craig (Skip) S. Humes
September, 1986

THE KEY TO CONVERSION

The gospel came into my life as a result of a crisis. I had married my high school sweetheart after his return from a tour of duty in the army. We had a beautiful, healthy baby daughter, Lori. When she was eight months old, my husband decided he was no longer in love and did not want to remain married. He left, taking with him my happiness and peace of mind. My deep depression began to nag at my sanity until I felt life was no longer worth living, and I began to entertain thoughts of suicide. I had had little religious training and had not learned the enormity of the sin of taking one's own life.

At this point, my only brother urged me to investigate the Church. He had been converted through a young girl he knew in high school.

"Carole, I know this will help you," he prompted.

"Nothing will help me," I responded with self-pity. I even laughed at the idea that "getting religion" could do anything for me.

Because of his love for me, my brother wept. My heart was immediately softened because I love him, too. I agreed, for his sake, to investigate.

The missionaries taught me to pray. From that time forward I gained a semblance of peace in my life, and though my problems were not immediately solved (our wise Father in Heaven knows we must, for the most part, solve our own problems), I gained the peace of mind and serenity to put my life in order. After nearly a year of frequent study and prayer, I knew the church was true. I was baptized at the Oakland Tri-stake Center March 26, 1960.

Though I knew the Church was true, was right for me, and would always be a force in my life, I was still not convinced of the necessity of a temple marriage when a new love entered my life.

Jim was a nonmember, smoked, drank moderately, and had very little religious background, though his parents were solid, honest, family-loving people. His stable family life contrasted greatly with my mother's two divorces and three marriages and the resultant insecurity of my young life. But just as instinctively as I knew the Church was true, so, too, did I know that Jim loved me as no one else did or ever would. I knew marrying him was as much a part of my salvation as joining the Church.

We were married on July 21, 1961, by the bishop of our ward. Within a year of our marriage, Jim began college. He had worked for seven years after high school graduation, but we both felt it best that he attend college to do the kind of work he really wanted. Though I had stressed my devotion to the Church, and told Jim that he would have to count on my attending Church twice every Sunday and at least one night a week (I served in Mutual), I had not made any ultimatums or requests of him other than that I expected him to seriously investigate the Church at some point—left undefined. When he began college, I realized he would want to put his education first, and it would be after his graduation from college before he could seriously consider the Church.

By the time Jim graduated from Humboldt State College in Arcata, California, we had three children, two sons (Mathew and Martin), being born to us in addition to Lori, whom Jim had adopted. He elected to go on for a master's degree and we moved to Reno, Nevada. I suffered a period of partial inactivity there—I worked at two or three part-time jobs to supplement Jim's assistantship salary, though I never did feel away from the Church.

While a graduate student, Jim came to the conclusion that smoking was an unhealthy and expensive habit and gave it up. I was thrilled as I felt it would be one less problem when he seriously investigated the Church.

After obtaining a master's degree, Jim accepted a job in Butte, Montana. There I became thoroughly involved in the Church and in due time was called to be president of the YWMIA. Our daughter, Julie, was born to us in Butte. Along with my increased activity came an increased desire to have our family together. I knew Jim was a very special person, and I wanted to extend our very special marriage into eternity.

I alternated between periods of great hope and staunch faith and the depths of discouragement. I read every article in the Church magazines looking for clues to my husband's conversion. There must be a key, I reasoned, a way to reach his spirituality. Though he wanted his family to have the benefits of Church membership and training, he felt it was not necessary for himself. I found very little written on the subject of part-member families until Elder Boyd K. Packer's article in the 1972 *Ensign*, "Begin Where You Are—At Home." I tried hard to live as much of the gospel as I could.

For years I tried to institute a family home evening in our home. Jim was only half-heartedly interested at first. We got a manual faithfully every year only to use one or two lessons out of it. At length Jim began to see the necessity for having family home evenings, but he chafed at using a structured program like the manual. When it was Jim's turn, he did his own thing. The children, likewise, usually planned an activity-type evening. But I began to notice something. Each year we seemed to use more and more of the manual. Gradually, Jim discovered its usefulness and the wisdom of using it. Over a period of about ten years, home evenings became regular Monday evening affairs, and it was Jim who pounded the table, declaring, "We cannot miss family home evening!"

Gathering a year's supply of food for storage was easy for Jim to accept. It appealed to his naturally prudent and cautious nature, and we budgeted and saved until we were able to accomplish this goal.

Meanwhile our children were growing. They all regularly attended their Church meetings. Our oldest daughter, Lori, gained an especially fervent testimony, and when she embroidered her sampler for Primary which said, "I will bring the light of the gospel into my home," she took it to heart and became a shining example.

Jim went to a meeting or social occasionally. I think he attended stake conforences more than anything else. He didn't really enjoy church when he went. Sometimes he made negative comments about the hymns, which he generally did not enjoy. Lori had started taking piano lessons the first year we moved to Butte. By the time she was in high school, her teacher, a member, assigned Church hymns. Since she practiced each morning, we became so familiar with the hymns Jim found himself humming them while he shaved. I smiled to myself and remembered that Elder Packer had said to make your husband feel at church while he's at home so he will feel at home when he's at church!

In December, 1974, our oldest son, Matt, became a deacon. A good family friend and hunting buddy invited Jim to attend priesthood with him one morning, and Jim went. The following Sunday morning our friend was away and didn't ask Jim to go, but he went anyway! He has missed only one or two priesthood meetings since that day.

On March 26, 1975, Jim was baptized and confirmed. He obtained the Aaronic Priesthood the next day. Within five months our stake president was calling S. Dilworth Young to inquire if Jim could be made an elder at our next stake conference. Permission was granted, and in August, 1975, Jim received the Melchizedek Priesthood. The following April 16, 1976, our family was sealed together in the Idaho Falls Temple. It was a glorious evening! I cannot think of it yet without tears of joy springing to my eyes.

Jim's conversion, of course, ultimately rested with himself, his recognition of the Holy Ghost, and his reliance on faith. However, two factors were helpful in preparing Jim for conversion: First, I made a point of accepting Jim for what he was, letting him know that I loved him no matter what, whether he joined the Church or not. After all, it was my decision to marry out of the church, and I knew he should not be made to feel he was in any way a disappointment to me. A man can sense your approval or disapproval. It was extremely important for me to accept full responsibility for my decision. Second, I realized that my first job was to worry about my own worthiness and progress in the gospel. This came about largely through a blessing I received at the hands of a spiritually sensitive bishop, after a youth conference. As YWMIA president and a chaperone, I returned home exhausted from the two nearly sleepless nights that seem to be an indispensable part of the youth conference experience. There was much to do at home on my return Saturday afternoon, so on Sunday morning I was still very tired and slept as late as I dared. I arose barely in time to get to an early morning mothers-and-daughters meeting for which I was responsible, but too late to give Jim and the children breakfast. He was angry when I left the house, and when I returned he was still angry. We exchanged harsh words, and my attendance at the three other scheduled meetings appeared impossible. I resolved to tell our bishop that not only could I not make the meetings, but that I was close to giving up all the activity in the Church, though this was not what Jim was asking of me.

In tears I went to Sunday School and sought out the bishop. He took one look at me and knew I had trouble. I tried to tell him something of the situation, but, surprisingly, he seemed to be expecting it. I learned later he had dreamed the night before that I would ask for my release. Inviting me into his office, he gave me the following blessing: "Sister Cole, I promise you, if you will do all the things you should do, Jim will be baptized." This gave me comfort, but I returned home still apprehensive about Jim's attitude. After apologizing for my failure to be a wife first and YWMIA president second, we were reconciled, and with Jim's approval I kept the rest of my schedule for the day.

As I thought about the blessing, I realized that the bishop did not say: "Go home and tell Jim to do this," or "Tell Jim he must do that." What he told me was what I had to do: Live the gospel—all of it!

My testimony has grown through Jim's conversion, not because of any one stunning inspiration or revelation, but because of many small insights gained through an effort to live the gospel, every bit of it. Others also living the gospel, using their priesthood and authority, and sharing their influence and spirituality have also touched our lives.

Now I know that there is only one key to *any problem* we face in our lives—*live the gospel with all your might, mind and strength.*

Carole Osborne Cole
September, 1987

GRATEFUL CONVERTS

My wife, our four children, and I joined The Church of Jesus Christ of Latter-day Saints on March 8, 1973. Our conversion to this only true church on earth was the most significant choice we ever made. When I look back over the past thirteen years, our blessings from knowing and living the gospel are unaccountable. We love the gospel teachings and are thankful for those missionaries who taught them to us. Our conversion story is simple but powerful.

Coming from a very traditional Chinese family, I was taught to worship my ancestors from the time I was a child and that if I respected them, I would receive blessings from them. Chinese people participate in rituals and ceremonies to show respect and honor to their ancestors. I must have attended some of these as a child, but do not recall them, and as an adult, I didn't practice them.

As I grew up I deeply respected my ancestors, but I didn't feel right worshiping them. Right after I graduated from high school, the political turmoil in my homeland was getting worse. Therefore, I fled from China to Hong Kong for life and freedom. When I got to Hong Kong, I was all alone, didn't know anyone, and didn't have any money. I was very lonely for my parents and others in China. I also worried about their safety. I worked all kinds of odd jobs to support myself and send money to my family.

As time went by, I began to establish my own family. On November 15, 1955, I married a lovely lady, Chan Yee Man, in Hong Kong. (In Chinese the surname precedes the given name.) Within three years our home was blessed with three adorable children: Lai Kwok To (Andrew), Lai Sau Kuen (Isabella), and Lai Fu To (Bruce). In 1962, another little girl blessed our lives. We named her Lai Mei Kuen (Michelle). They are all most important and precious to me. I love them dearly. I wanted to provide the best for them including a college education because I loved school and didn't have a chance to go to college myself.

My wife was a member of the Anglican church, and our children often attended with her on Sunday. Church was a new subject to me. I didn't know what it was and didn't really care. However, I liked my family to attend as it provided good activities for them.

My first contact with LDS missionaries was twenty years ago. At that time I was about thirty-five and owned a small textile factory. Two meek, polite, and clean-cut American boys came to my door on a hot summer day. They wanted to tell me their church's teachings. I was very impressed with them, so I let them teach me. Thereafter, every time they came I listened to them, not because I was interested in their church doctrine, but simply because I liked them. I thought it must be very hard for these two young boys to live in a strange land so far from their families.

Later, they didn't come any more because I wasn't willing to be baptized into the Church. Besides, my wife felt uncomfortable being involved in another church since she had her own faith.

Nineteen Seventy-three was a very bad year for many people in Hong Kong. A lot of stockholders lost money because their stocks fell rapidly, myself included. Suddenly I was bankrupt! In a month I lost all my stocks and my textile factory. I became very depressed. I blamed myself for buying so many stocks. I felt I didn't do my family any good. That year we lived by selling machines and tools that were left in the factory.

Then a miracle came in October. Some other young missionaries came back! I hadn't seen any for seven years. When Elder Ronald Richins and Elder Perschon came to my door, I felt they were old friends. As we sat around the table, I listened to them tell the story of Joseph Smith. After they finished, I invited them to have dinner with my family. They told us about the family home evening program and said they would have one with us the following visit. My family liked the idea.

Our first family home evening was very beautiful. Elder Richins made a clever board for the occasion. We thought it must have taken him a lot of time to do the board and that must mean he really cared for us. The missionaries taught us to pray and to sing "There Is Beauty All Around." We loved the song. During the meeting, we played a game to see how much my children knew. I liked that. This game built my self-esteem as the father of the home. From that night on, they came every week to teach the gospel. For some reason, my wife and children liked them a lot, too. Every time they came, my children would watch for them through the windows as they approached our house.

At that time we were humble and prepared to accept the gospel. We didn't doubt the doctrines but believed God's plan of salvation, the mission of our Savior Jesus Christ, the restoration of the gospel by the priesthood of God through the Prophet Joseph Smith. We believed the commandments, that the Book of Mormon was the word of God as well as were the beautiful messages explained to us. We had a testimony and felt happy and that it was right for us to be baptized.

After we became members, we wanted to keep all the commandments as well as we could. My wife and I never smoked or drank before we joined which made it easer to live the teachings in that respect. As I regained my self-confidence, I started to look for a suitable business opportunity. My wife and I used our last savings to buy a little shop. We thought selling clothes in it would give us a good profit. However, we decided to take turns attending church meetings on Sunday and thus make more profit by not closing our shop on the Sabbath. As a result, everything went wrong in the family. We were frustrated. At last I sought help from Heavenly Father. I wanted to know what I could do to make my family happy. I was prompted by the Holy Ghost that I should close the store. I realized I could lose my last bit of money by doing that, but from that day we closed the store and we never missed a church meeting on Sunday.

I didn't know what was ahead for us. One day while walking along the street feeling hopelessness, I met an old friend. During our conversation, he invited me to join him and and two other friends to open an oil company which sold industrial oil to factories. I was able to borrow some money and start in this business with them. It has been a great blessing to my family. Heavenly Father blessed this business that my four children could finish college, and three of them served a full-time mission for the Church. I doubt that I could have provided a college education for them if I had only owned the clothing shop. A couple of years ago the economy was not stable in Hong Kong, and many oil companies closed down, but not ours.

Our testimonies of the gospel continue to grow as we keep the commandments and serve in the Church. When the Taipei Taiwan Temple was opened, I took my wife to it on February 20, 1985, to have our temple marriage and to be sealed to each other for time and all eternity. On December 17, 1986, again in this temple, our four children were sealed to us for all eternity. This temple blessing was the biggest goal we have achieved. We did it, we enjoyed it, and we were thankful for it. One of the great highlights at this time was to have Elder Jerry Craner, who helped teach the gospel after Elder Richins, with us when we were sealed as a family.

I have a strong testimony of the gospel, as do my wife and children, and we strive to live every principle of it. Our great hope is to share it with others. We feel that living the gospel gives us the strength, faith, and power to rise above adversity and look beyond the present-day troubles to a brighter day.

Hoi Nam Lai
Stake Patriarch in the
Kowloon Hong Kong North Stake
February 15, 1986

PROUD TO BE DESCENDANT
OF THE PROPHET

My conversion story is so simple that I find it amazing that people are as affected by it as they are. Perhaps it is because they are surprised to learn that the Prophet Joseph Smith's family was not in the Church but had to come in through convert baptism.

After Joseph and Hyrum Smith's martyrdom, the Church eventually moved westward under the direction of Brigham Young. Hyrum's wife, Mary Fielding Smith, took her family West, but the Prophet Joseph's wife, Emma, remained in the East. When people ask me why Mary had the courage to go and Emma did not, I reply somewhat defensively for Emma's sake: "Mary was younger and had Hyrum's grown sons to help her. Emma was forty years old and five months into her eighth pregnancy when Joseph died. She buried seven babies of her own and one adopted child. Her eldest child, Julia, was not quite fifteen; young Joseph was not yet twelve; Frederick was eight; and Alexander Hale Smith was only six years old. The baby, born in November after his father's death, was named David Hyrum. He was not a robust child and was only two years old when the Church left Nauvoo in the middle of the winter. Emma had already crossed the Mississippi twice on the ice, while fleeing persecution. Her 'failure' to come West seems to stand as an ugly blemish on her character, but to her it seemed the only logical course to take. In later years when she was asked why she did not go West, she said that it was because she knew what she had there in Nauvoo and she did not know what lay 'out there.' "

Her decision has had far reaching effects on her posterity. For more than half a century, not one of her descendants was in the Church. During that time bitter prejudice was bred into the family against Brigham Young and the Church in Utah.

In the 1930s, my grandfather, Louis Hurst Horner, moved his family from Lamoni, Iowa, to Nebraska, then to Wyoming, and finally to northwestern Montana where he established a farm at Ronan, Montana. His wife, Coral Smith Horner, was the ninth child of Alexander Hale Smith, Joseph's third living son. With this move, a branch of Joseph's family was separated from the center of the Reorganized Church's influence. As there was no Reorganized Church near enough for her to attend, Grandmother reared her four children without specific religious doctrine or church affiliation, though the family members were all devout Christians and usually attended the community Protestant church at Round Butte, or the Methodist Church in Ronan.

Their youngest child, Lorene, is my mother. She was a teenager when the family moved to Ronan. She finished high school and married a native Montanan, Rupert Normandeau, who was of French Canadian ancestry. He was also a member of the Flathead Indian tribe.

They had four children, three girls and a boy. I am the second child in the family. Growing up on the reservation, I had no knowledge of my Smith ancestry.

In fact, I never heard the word Mormon or saw a copy of the Book of Mormon until I was 17.

I did not know I was related to a man named Joseph Smith until I went to school. Since Mother had been persecuted as a child and she didn't want me to suffer the same way, she admonished me not to tell anyone I was related to him.

The summer before my junior year in high school, my father took a job in the eastern part of the state at Conrad, Montana. We moved from the reservation and rented a small farmhouse from Lederers, ranchers in the area. I also babysat for them. When I started working, my mother warned, "Don't tell Dee Lederer you are related to Joseph Smith or she will think you should be a Mormon." This is the first time I recall hearing the word Mormon. I had no idea what a Mormon was or what connection it had with Joseph Smith. I was extremely curious. Therefore, I disobeyed my mother, asking Dee to tell me who Joseph Smith was and finally telling her I was related to him somehow.

Her reaction was just what my mother had feared. She explained that he had founded The Church of Jesus Christ of Latter-day Saints which is sometimes called the Mormon Church. Indeed she did think I should be a Mormon, and she introduced me to the missionaries, who lived in her basement apartment in Conrad, (Elder Dean Richins from Arizona and Elder James Waldron from Malad, Idaho).

One day I stopped at Dee's house after school. As I entered the kitchen, Dee told me the missionaries had a little gift for me. I couldn't imagine why they, complete strangers to me, should want to give me a present. The elders were standing side by side waiting for me to enter. Elder Waldron held out a small black book with a tiny gold embossed picture on the front.

"This is a copy of the Book of Mormon," he said. "It was translated by your great-great-grandfather, and it is true."

The most incredible feeling came over me as I curled my fingers around the book. My mind seemed infused with a burning sense of knowing. "This is true! This is true!" I thought.

I took the book home and began to read it. It was so interesting to me that I couldn't put it down. Noticing my constant reading, my father asked me, "What is that you're reading?" When I replied that it was the Book of Mormon, he got a strange look on his face and said gravely, "Don't dig too deep. Don't dig too deep!" But he didn't tell me I couldn't read the book, so I continued and finished it in a short time.

The next thing I realized was that I had a strong desire to know more about the Church. Again my parents were reluctant about my being drawn into something they did not wholly approve. Yet, they permitted me to take the missionary lessons. They both abhorred prejudice and wanted us children to make up our own minds about religion.

However, when I asked for permission to be baptized, their tolerance dissolved. My father's answer was, "Not under my roof." Mother and I argued over the subject and got nowhere. Only when I was 18 and moved out of the house was I baptized. This memorable event occurred on March 17, 1956, in Great Falls, Montana. I was baptized by Elder Beecham from St. Augustine, Florida. I did not know at the time, but learned later that I was the first of Joseph Smith's descendants to come into the Church and stay.

That was over thirty years ago. I have reared a family of my own, traveled and lectured at hundreds of firesides, and am presently writing a trilogy which will stand as my written testimony. *Emma's Glory and Sacrifice* is a testimony of the legacy I feel I received from my great-great-grandmother, Emma. *What Happened to the Family of the Prophet Joseph Smith* is an explanation of how the Prophet's family became estranged from the Church and the testimonies of three family members who have been converted. The third book, *Unmasking the Prejudice,* reveals some of the misunderstandings that have divided the family from the true faith through the past hundred years and invites all who hold prejudice against the Church to cast off the cloak of miunderstanding and look for truth without fear.

My father passed away in 1964. My mother joined the Church in Charlo, Montana, in 1979. She served a full-time mission for the Church, being the first of Joseph Smith's descendants ever to serve as a missionary. There are now fifty-five descendants of Joseph and Emma in the Church. Twelve of them are converts; the others are second- and third-generation members.

I find joy in the principles of the gospel of Jesus Christ as they have been restored through my great-great-grandfather, Joseph Smith. I delight in learning the Lord's commandments from the scriptures. I listen earnestly to the living prophets and love to obey their counsel. I truly enjoy serving the Church in whatever capacity I am called. In short, I rejoice in the knowledge of a loving, caring, personal Father in Heaven, and I am humbly grateful for the atonement of his Son, our Savior, Jesus Christ.

Gracia N. Jones
August, 1986

LOVED INTO THE GOSPEL

I was born and lived twenty-two years in Geneva, Switzerland, before coming to the United States.

My childhood memories are happy, although I was an only child and often wished I could have a brother or sister. My cousin, Monique, was born about three hours before me, and we grew up together almost as sisters.

After high school, I attended business school for two years and then went to England to become more fluent in English. Returning home, I worked for the Swiss Telephone Company. I enjoyed my work very much as I spoke to people from Germany, England, Italy, and occasionally the United States. I also worked at the United Nations when several world leaders met for important conferences. My work there was mostly public relations, translating messages for journalists attending the conference, and helping them telephone their home office.

In February, 1955, while skiing in Davos, I met a young American soldier stationed in Nance, France. He was visiting Switzerland, the native land of his maternal grandmother, Mary Emma Schreier Biron. As in fairy tales, it was love at first sight. After only four days, he asked me to marry him, and I accepted.

We talked endlessly it seemed. Burton told me all about his family and of his Mormon religion which was totally new to me. Religion, however, took second place in my thoughts. My main concern was that I would have to leave my family and native land. Since we had known each other for such a short time, we decided to delay marriage and write to each other for a year.

Back at his base in France, Burton obtained special premission to come to Geneva where he met my parents and asked for my hand in marriage. My whole family was impressed. They felt at ease around him, loved him, and trusted him. We wrote many letters, and when our feelings were still the same at the end of the year, we decided to get married. It had been a hard decision to make, not only for me, but also for my parents.

We were married on May 26, 1956; two days later, I said good-bye to my parents, other relatives, and friends. We then boarded a plane for New York. Leaving was definitely difficult, but I felt happy and confident as Burton's bride.

From New York where Burton had left his car, we drove home to Evanston, Wyoming, where his family welcomed me warmly and were kind and helpful. I immediately felt a part of Burton's family. I began to attend church regularly and was warmly received there. Soon I was enjoying many new friendships.

The gospel of Jesus Christ as taught by the Church was a wonder to me. I found in it the same vastness that had so impressed me in this land. Little by little, I settled into my new life, homesick sometimes, but happy. Burton was kind and loving. Not only did he have a great sense of humor, he was a tease as well, telling me for instance, that strawberry shortcake was called strawberry longcake. I believed him, but only for a while.

After four years, two children, and hearing the missionary lessons twice, I was baptized a member of Burton's faith. Learning of our pre-earth life and of the plan of life and salvation made a deep impression on me. Having been Protestant, I had some knowledge of a life after death, but nothing compared to gospel teachings. Eternal marriage and family were what I really wanted, yet I still had some reservations about my baptism because I felt my knowledge of such a great religion was inadequate. Finally I became convinced that baptism had to be my first step. My husband, who had been very understanding and patient, baptized and confirmed me on May 2, 1959. It was a special occasion, not only for us but for our children, Burton's family, and many friends.

I first taught Primary and attended Sunday School classes. I learned a great deal from both. Two years later, on May 5, 1961, Burton and I were sealed for time and all eternity in the Salt Lake Temple. At this time our three children, Eric, Kim, and Cindy were sealed to us, Cindy having been born after I was baptized.

I will never forget how beautiful the children looked. The Lord was giving me many blessings. Tears of true joy welled up in my eyes. It was a wonderful experience, made even more special and meaningful because of family members in attendance.

Six years later, our fourth child, Clay, was born the day after Christmas. He brought our family a lot of happiness and fun. Our three older children delighted in playing with and tending him. As time went on, I had many more opportunities to hold various positions in the Church, and I always received much more than I gave. As a result, my testimony and knowledge of the gospel grew.

During all these years, I kept in close touch with my parents and relatives. My mother was with me when our first baby was born. She stayed four months, and I still have wonderful memories of that special time. About seven years later, when we moved into our new home, my father and mother came and stayed ten months. Their visit was a most enjoyable time for all of us. They got to know our three chidren and became acquainted with Burton's family and our way of life. Eight years later, I took my first trip back home. From then on, I was able to go more often and visit my parents who were ailing. My father passed away, and two years later, Mother died.

I think of them often. I appreciate their love and unselfishness in letting me make my home far away from them, for surely they must have been lonely at times. Twice I had the missionaries talk to them, but they never chose to join the Church. In due time after their deaths, Burton and I performed temple ordinances for my father, Marcel Pierre Schmid, and my mother, Cecile Louise Berset Schmid. It was a privilege to do their temple work, for I had wanted them to have the blessings of the gosepl. Now they could have them, and this assurance and knowledge gave me a warm and wonderful feeling.

In recent years, we have had the blessing and privilege of seeing our three oldest children marry in the temple. We have also performed ordinances for other family members. Another blessing has been the visits of several members of my family, among them, my cousin Monique. Despite the many miles of separation, we share close ties.

Through the tragedy of losing our youngest son, Clay, in a timber accident, October 28, 1985, the significance of the concept of the eternal family has become even more important to us. Clay was preparing and looking forward to going on a mission. Losing him has been a great test of faith and, at times, harder to endure than we felt capable of. But we *can* find comfort in the teachings of the gospel, that life continues after death and our loved ones are not far from us. They know and care for us. The gospel of Jesus Christ is indeed the light that will guide us back to our Heavenly Father and loved ones if we live according to his principles and ordinances. Everything in the gospel is for our benefit. If we meet our trials with faith, humility, patience, and trust in the Lord, he will, as promised, bless us and reunite us with those we love and miss. I marvel at the blessings in store for us predicated upon our faithfuless and obedience. The gospel has taught me a great deal, but more specifically, it has taught me about the Savior. His infinite love and his ultimate sacrifice which, by conquering death, opened the doors of salvation and eternal life for us.

I love the Lord and thank him for all my blessings, for my loving husband, our wonderful children who are close to us, our beautiful and precious grandchildren, and a family who literally loved me into the gospel by example. I am grateful for the gift of life itself, the gospel, the knowledge of where I came from and my purpose on earth. I also appreciate the opportunity of doing genealogy research for my family and offering them gospel blessings.

Since the loss of our son, I have learned to appreciate the principle of prayer which enables me to communicate with and draw closer to my Heavenly Father. God lives. He loves us, answers our prayers, and gives us strength to endure our trials. I pray that with his divine help, I will always remain faithful, endure to the end and once again have our dear Clay and my family forever.

Evelyne J. South
December 12, 1986

LOOKING BACK

Looking back at events in the past decade that led us to the LDS Church, my wife, Diane, and I are amazed at how the hand of the Lord has shaped our lives. We have often said that we backed into the Church because we were involved in church-related activities without really understanding Mormon doctrine.

Some ten years ago, before it was popular, we began to work on our genealogy. Since we were interested in pre-Civil War U.S. history, this seemed a natural extension of our study. We made several trips to the East Coast, compiling many records. Diane had been using the LDS Library in Dearborn, Michigan, to run microfilm she had ordered from Salt Lake City. It never occurred to her that the librarian was LDS. One day, in passing conversation, the librarian told Diane, "Sometime ask a Mormon why they do genealogy."

One afternoon in the summer of 1975, two young missionaries knocked at our door. They asked if they could come some evening and talk about the family. Diane said they were welcome any evening, but to call first. We never heard from them again, and we moved soon afterward. Perhaps the Lord knew we weren't yet ready to hear their story, but seeds were being planted.

By the fall of 1977, our daughter, Kari, was three years old and her brother, Kevin, had just been born. At this point the hand of the Lord began to take an active role in our lives. We became increasingly more uncomfortable with organized religion. Our study of the Bible reinforced our belief that churches taught only man's adaptation of God's doctrine. Although we had been lifetime Methodists, we felt that God's true church would offer more than we were receiving. In an effort not to confuse our children, we decided to spend our Sundays teaching them what we believed to be the truth.

During this same period, I applied for several transfers that should have materialized; but circumstances would not allow us, for one reason or another, to accept one. All these jobs would have taken us to other parts of the state. All should have taken place, yet none did. We began to question what was happening to us. Then a telephone call turned our lives upside down. A man in my company had passed away unexpectedly which necessitated a replacement, and I was their choice. Diane and I had only 12 hours to make up our minds. The transfer would take me to my hometown of Midland, Michigan, the one place my lovely wife had vowed never to move.

Events surrounding the transfer were remarkable. A transfer had never been offered under such conditions. It was normal procedure for interested applicants to apply and interview; but in this case, the company disregarded their regular channels and contacted me directly. Our house sold to the first person who looked at it in a market where houses had been for sale as long as two years. We were able to purchase a new home with just as much ease, and real estate brokers on both sides were amazed. Everything fell into place like the pieces of a puzzle. We realized we were moving to Midland for a reason.

Our thoughts about religion weighed heavily upon us after the move. One evening while wandering through the public library, we found ourselves in the religion section. My eyes fell upon the Book of Mormon. I told Diane I wanted to read it, and she selected a book from the same shelf entitled *A Marvelous Work and A Wonder* by LeGrand Richards. At the time, we didn't realize the books were connected in any way. Together, we poured through the books, often until after 1 a.m., discussing what we had read.

During this time, Diane had also been reading a book by Howard J. Ruff entitled, *How to Prosper During the Coming Bad Years.* The book aroused our interest in developing a food storage program. We had experienced tornado-like winds the previous year in Plymouth that left us without power for five days in 100-degree heat. The experiece gave us a true sense of our lack of preparation. The book outlined a storage program and referred readers interested in purchasing wheat to the president of the Relief Society The Church of Jesus Christ of Latter-day Saints. We didn't learn until much later that Mr. Ruff was also a Mormon.

Eager to begin our program, Diane went to the phone directory and found that a Church bishop, Robert Pommerville, lived just around the corner from us. Diane called and inquired of his wife, Arlene, what course we might take in acquiring wheat. Arlene put us in contact with the proper people and, in the process of many telephone calls, we felt a great friendship developing.

One evening when Bob and Arlene stopped by the house to see our Vita-Mix grind wheat, we asked them questions about Church doctrine. I think they were amazed when we told them we were reading the Book of Mormon and *A Marvelous Work and A Wonder.*

Arlene told us that she knew "two cute little missionaries" who could answer our questions and felt that the practice would do them good. She asked if they could come by and we agreed. (I think those seeds that had been planted were developing into small plants.)

We spent many hours with Elders Shurtliff and Brady and Elders Dunn and Rasmussen. Often our sessions lasted from 1:00 or 2:00 in the afternoon until their curfew that night. Those poor elders must have wondered what they had gotten themselves into. I think they knew they were loved and welcome in our home. Besides, we always fed them well. They taught us the lessons and answered questions we had compiled over several years of study.

At the prompting of the missionaries, I had prayed earnestly about the truthfulness of the Book of Mormon. I received an answer so overwhelmingly strong I could barely control my enthusiasm. Diane couldn't believe I had made a decision like this so quickly. It was completely out of character for me. In the two years we had been looking at churches, I had always made decisions slowly, with much deliberation, and now, suddenly this. She felt I had totally and completely lost it and told me so. The missionaries had more lessons for us, and she said she would make no commitment until she had heard everything. And let me emphasize EVERYTHING!

I, on the other hand, had been so moved by the Spirit that I was nearly driving the poor woman crazy. I questioned her at every opportunity to see if she had made a decision. The moment she awoke, at lunch, during walks in the evening, before bed, I didn't miss a chance. Through it all, she still put up with me.

Then something very dramatic happened to us. One night the next week, I had a vivid dream which appeared to be in color. In my dream, I was in a circular room with numerous doors. I was instructed to open the first, where I saw myself. I had lost my job and was applying everywhere imaginable, confidently looking for work. Behind the second door, I saw my family doing without. Behind the third, I saw that we were no longer in our home. We had moved to a very tiny house, much in need of repair. The doors continued. I saw the situation worsen over what appeared to be not weeks, but years. I saw the values we had taught our children deteriorate. I saw tears and extreme poverty. I saw myself with nowhere to turn for either the spiritual or physical needs of my family. When I could bear it no more, I knelt down in the room and cried. Suddenly, what seemed to be a voice said, "You weren't prepared."

I awoke with sweat at 5:00 a.m. I paced throughout the house and prayed and paced some more. At 6:00 a.m., Diane noticed I was gone and came to find me. I told her I had a frightening dream. "That's odd," she said, "I had a really strange dream, too, and I never remember my dreams." She asked me to tell her about the dream. I did and told her again of my feelings towards the Church. When I had finished, she looked at me with tears in her eyes and said, "Dan, in my dream there was a room. You and I were there. I was looking at you, but you couldn't see me. As I looked at you, what seemed to be a voice said to me, "Trust him." Then I awoke and noticed you were gone.

We both knew our lives had been touched by the Holy Spirit. We knew that our decision to join the Church had been made. It was time to harvest those seeds planted so many years ago. We were baptized two weeks later, August 4, 1982.

During the next year, we experienced growth individually and as a family while preparing to go to the temple. On August 27, 1983, we traveled to the Washigton, D.C. Temple where we received those great blessings and promises, the fulfillment of which would depend upon our faithfulness. Diane and I were joined by Kari and Kevin at the altar where we were sealed together for time and all eternity. What greater blessing could our Father in Heaven have given us than this?

The Church has become an active source of strength and guidance in our lives. We have participated in many Church activities and have accepted various callings. Church service has resulted in many blessings for our family.

On January 9, 1984, my father, Norman W. Miller, passed away. What great comfort our knowledge of the truth of the gospel has been. Even though there is sadness at his passing, the sure knowledge of the Lord's plan of salvation has greatly lightened this burden. Knowing that one year from now I can do temple ordinances for my father to help him even after he has departed this earth has brought us peace and joy.

Our Father in Heaven guides and directs our lives if we let him. If we but listen to the still small voice of the Holy Ghost, the truth of the gospel will be made known to us. We testify of the truth of the gospel and The Church of Jesus Christ of Latter-day Saints. We pray that each of your lives may be filled with the joy that only knowing the Lord can bring.

Dan and Diane Miller

MY FAVORITE SUBJECT

I love to talk about experiences that led me to a sure knowledge that The Church of Jesus Christ of Latter-day Saints is the only true church. I make this claim not boastfully, but humbly, for the joy and happiness membership has brought.

I grew up in Canada and always felt proud and fortunate to have Victor Krausz and Nora Irene Sturm as my parents. They are good German people. Their parents also spoke German but because of the constant struggle going on between German and Russian boundaries, they were actually born in Russia. This situation makes research on my ancestors interesting and often very challenging.

Dad was very active, loved life, and played a banjo by ear. While he never had a music lesson in his life, he played in dance bands for years. He especially enjoyed hunting, fishing, sports, traveling, and collecting rare coins, stamps, and rocks. Mother has rare qualities, too. She is extremely amibitous. She seems to have as much energy as three women combined. She likes people and is interested in them.

Mother was eighteen and Father was twenty-six when they were married in 1936, during the Depression. She recalls that it was the first time in her life she had a dress purchased at a store!

As I was growing up, Dad and Mom operated a business on the trans-Canada highway. It consisted of a grocery store, cabins, a service station, lunch counter, and the only telephone in town at that time. We lived in the same area as the business so we served customers twenty-four hours a day, seven days a week. We often had dancing parties in our home up to three nights a week. Mother prepared food for all who came. She danced until 3:00 or 4:00 a.m. and then started working early the next day. I doubt she ever missed a dance. Dad enjoyed dancing, too, but he helped provide the music, playing his banjo.

While my parents didn't belong to, or attend any particular church, they were religious people and maintained proper values. They were almost fanatical about some things. When I pick up a pair of scissors on the Sabbath, I still remember Mother scolding me in German: "If you sew on Sunday, you will have to unpick those stitches in heaven with your nose." I spoke German and very little English until I was in the first grade. I still understand German when I am around Mom.

I was fourteen before I heard the word *Mormon*. A young family moved into our home-town of Walsh, Alberta, Canada. Maizie and her nonmember husband, Lee Crypko, had six children. Soon everyone who came to our store or service station knew that "Mormons" were in town. Not wanting to admit my ignorance, I looked for what made Mormons different. Maizie was young, but her hair had turned completely grey, so I assumed this was one of the signs. I was attracted to her at once, and over the next four years, we were drawn to each other.

Father was very strict, allowing me few freedoms. I rarely disobeyed him because I knew I would get a whipping.

In January, 1957, after my eighteenth birthday, I was a bit brave and asked his permission to go to church with Maizie. (The nearest LDS Church was in Medicine Hat, 33 miles away.) I was not surprised when Dad said, "No, you may not go!" I went anyway, knowing I would be punished later.

That was the first of a lifetime of events that changed my life for eternity. I had a feeling of love and acceptance that night I had never felt before. This warm and comfortable feeling felt good to my soul. Like everyone else, I had a deep need to be loved. I constantly yearned for my dad to tell me he loved me. The Saints in that little chapel transmitted their love to me as though it were magic. It was wonderful.

I did a rather foolish thing that first night which seems amusing to me now. I wore a little brown hat with yellow daisies on each side. Since this was not the custom in that branch, they immediately knew I was an investigator.

The Holy Ghost bore witness to me that the teachings I heard there were true. I wanted to learn more. Although I was ecstatic over this grand experience, the events that followed were not all pleasant. In the coming days, Dad and I had many bitter words. One Sunday afternoon as I was leaving, he stood within my reach, beads of perspiration on his chalk-white face as he made his final announcement, "Lorraine, if you join the Mormon Church, you will no longer be a child of mine."

I walked out, got on a Greyhound bus, and went to Medicine Hat. There I roomed and boarded with a little elderly lady, Mrs. Singer. Luckily, I soon obtained employment with the Alberta Government Telephone as a telephone operator.

I started meeting weekly with some LDS missionaries who taught me a series of lessons. I knew beyond a shadow of a doubt that their gospel teachings were true. It was bitter-sweet, for I realized my father had disowned me. Mom did write, and I answered her, sending my letters to her neighbor. Another heartbreaking experience was to leave my ten-year-old sister, Peggy, behind.

On June 2, 1957, I was baptized and confirmed at Medicine Hat, Alberta, Canada, after waiting six *long* months for my parents' permission. It was a beautiful and special day. Maizie and I cried. Many members commented that I had a new look, that after my baptism my physical appearance changed. I felt the Spirit, and a sweet and calm feeling filled my soul that was truly marvelous. The only thing that could have made it more glorious was to have had Dad, Mom, and Peggy present.

My dear friend, Maizie, said to me more than once, "I was angry and disappointed when we moved to Walsh. But I now realize why the Lord had us move. It was my mission to help bring you the gospel, Lorraine."

During the next two years I tried three times to have Dad accept me back into the family, but each time was refused. He'd say, "If you will give up the Mormon Church and quit your job, you may return home." Of course, I couldn't!

In October, 1957, while I was working at the Alberta telephone office as head cashier, a couple of new elders came in to pay a telephone bill. I immediately knew they were LDS missionaries because they were wearing ties, hats, and white shirts. This seemed to amaze them. That was the first time I met Elder James H.

Steel from Rexburg, Idaho. He had eight months left to serve. After laboring six weeks in Medicine Hat, he was transferred to Calgary. I received three letters from him before he was released to go home.

His romance prior to his mission fell through, and he wrote to ask if I would go with him to the Calgary Stampede. He brought his cousin, J. C. Steel, and with his cousin's permission I arranged a date for him. The four of us had a grand time. This date was followed by an exciting courtship. Jim came to Canada several times.

We were married August 13, 1958, in the Idaho Falls Temple. We had a reception at Plano, near Rexburg, and two days later, one in the branch in Canada I had attended. Mom and Peggy came, but not my dad.

Some time later when Jim and I were expecting our first baby (J. Chesley), we made a trip to Canada. I asked Dad if he could forgive me for all the heartache and trouble I had caused him. He said, "Yes, I forgive you." We again commenced our relationship as a family. Dad seemed to like Jim, so did Mom and Peggy. They all adored Chesley, as well as our other three children, Bret, Kami, and Cozette, and have been exceptionally good to them.

In 1965 my parents took Jim and me on a vacation to California. It was the first time I had been on a trip with them, a truly memorable experience. We take so much for granted in our short lives on earth.

About ten years before Dad passed away, he and Mom sold their business and retired. They moved to Medicine Hat where Peggy and her son and daughter resided. Occasionally, they all visited us, and we went home at least once a year. We appreciated the times they went to church with us in Idaho and that they came for our son Bret's mission testimonial.

This past May, 1985, I attended church at Medicine Hat for the first time there in twenty-eight years. There were then three wards instead of the little branch of sixty when I joined the Church.

I always felt a strong need to have Dad tell me just once that he loved me. Many years later when I was forty-one and he was on his death bed at the age of sixty-nine, dying with cancer, he finally whispered, "I love you. I love you." This was a lifelong dream fulfilled, and I can hardly believe it to this day. Why are these words so difficult to say when our dear Savior displayed his constant love to each of us so freely?

I am saddened that none of my family has joined the Church. I have a constant prayer that their hearts will be touched and they will want to know and understand the gospel of Jesus Christ.

My friends, Maizie and Lee, divorced. She and their children moved to the United States where Maizie met and married Parley Davis. He was called to be a bishop in Salt Lake in 1980, and Jim and I spent this great occasion with them. Little did we know that within a few months we would call them to say Jim had been called as bishop of the Parker Idaho Ward, near St Anthony. Another moment we want to take with us into eternity was when Maizie and Parley met us at the Salt Lake Temple on August 3, 1983, when Chesley and his sweetheart, Kristine Erickson, were married.

I want each of our children to know how much I love them and that I love the Lord; that I know God lives, and hears and answers our prayers; that He truly loves us. I am grateful to be a member of the only true church. I love the Prophet Joseph Smith. I know we have a true prophet on the earth today. He will guide us if only we will follow his counsel. I am most grateful for the Book of Mormon, another testament to the Bible and of Jesus Christ, and that it is also a guide to us today. I want our children to realize that if I could leave them or share with them the greatest gift of all, it would be to be involved and engrossed in the true love of Christ through service to God and their fellowmen and to constantly strive for a strong testimony of their own. That is a gift directly from God to each of us but which cannot be given until each of us is ready for this gift.

Lorraine Steel
May, 1985

SPARED FOR A PURPOSE

I was born July 7, 1915, in Oldham, Lancashire, England, the youngest of eight children born to Morris and Elizabeth Buckley King. I was reared Episcopalian. My father was our church organist for forty years.

After school, I moved to London to work. I married Sidney Axtell in 1939. We had two children, John and Pauline, during the second world war. While my husband served in the king's army, I prepared meals for workers who built aircraft. The children and I slept in underground air raid shelters at night.

In 1954, Sidney was killed in a traffic accident. I later married Bill Blair, a Scotsman from Glasgow. We worked hard to provide the children with a good education.

Bill died in 1968 following a lengthy battle with cancer. I endured a long period of sadness and loneliness following his death.

In 1969, while returning from a visit to my daughter in Wales, my car slid on black ice and I was thrown through the windshield. Later I learned that I had actually been taken to the mortuary. Just as the mortician was about to cover my face preparing me for burial, a policeman saw one of my eyelids move. They quickly took me to the operating room, where surgeons performed a tracheotomy. I spent three months in the hospital recovering from multiple injuries. Since then, I have had great difficulty with breathing. It took a long time to regain my speech, and I still have trouble communicating. At this time, I had an insurance job with the government. Clients from South Africa, my territory, used to call and ask for "the lady with the broken tongue."

I decided to visit my sister, Elizabeth Murray, and her daughter, Jackie Richardson, in Jackson, Wyoming, in September, 1975. Another sister, Nellie Howarth, tried to talk me out of going, thinking I still wasn't well enough to travel alone. When she learned that I was flying as far as Salt Lake City with a group of Latter-day Saints on their way to general conference, she was especially concerned. She felt they would be a bad influence. But I could not be dissuaded. When I arrived at London's Heathrow Airport to board my flight, our group was told that our names weren't on the passenger list and we would have to wait. Later in our hotel, we learned that the flight organizer had absconded with our money. Our four-day wait for insurance reimbursement and another flight was not unpleasant for me. Most of the twenty-one other waiting passengers were members of the Church, and during that time I learned much.

For some years I had been searching for a truth that would explain the purpose of life and give me hope for the hereafter. In the last several years, I had begun to despair about religion. I had asked myself many times why a man as kind and thoughtful as Bill was allowed to suffer as he did. I was desperately trying to find the true gospel of Jesus Christ. I felt that if I did, these questions would be answered. I was deeply moved and awed by what these Church members told me. They answered each question with sincerity. I knew instantly that this was the gospel for which I had been searching. When I told them about my accident, they said that my life had been spared for a purpose. The feeling that this was true persisted and was so strong that I wanted to be baptized at once. But I felt I ought to first learn more about the Church. Everyone was extemely kind to me those four days. When we finally boarded our plane for Salt Lake City, one of the brethren asked the pilot if he could offer a prayer for our safety. I was impressed when the pilot mentioned this prayer upon our arrival, saying that the flight had gone especially well.

As far as I knew, no one would meet me at the airport. I was concerned about finding my way due to my speech problem. A Brother Jenner, another passenger, assured me that he had prayed for me and felt that someone would be there to meet me. Sure enough, Jackie and her husband, Weldon T. Richardson, Jr., were waiting there when I arrived. They drove me to Jackson.

Later, Jackie and Weldon, members of the Church, took me to sacrament meeting. There I met Bishop Murland May, a widower. We spent time together and talked about the Church. He arranged for me to attend general conference with him. I felt spiritually uplifted at conference. I felt that my Father in Heaven had indeed allowed me to be born again. I knew my life had been spared in that accident so I could be a missionary and spread the gospel.

My trip to Jackson was a turning point in my life. I arrived on September 14, 1975. Murland baptized me October 10, and we were married October 16, 1975. A year after our civil marriage, we were sealed for time and eternity in the Salt Lake Temple by Elder Mark E. Petersen.

On each of our eight trips to England, Murland and I have taken and distributed several copies of the Book of Mormon. We often talk to others about the

Church. I have told my children about the principles of the gospel, but so far neither has joined. However, I feel certain that my father accepted the gospel in the spirit world. When I was sealed to my parents in the temple we had a right good feeling, a proper good feeling about him.

Because of my breathing difficulties, I have had at least sixteen brushes with death in the last several years. Each time I have been revived and been able to continue enjoying life and serving the Lord. Murland and I have visited the London Temple three times together, performing a number of endowments for the dead. On October 7, 1986, we did twenty sealings in the Idaho Falls Temple.

I know God lives and blesses me. I know he preserved my life for a purpose.

Ada May
September, 1986

(Editor's note: While this book was being compiled, Ada May passed away due to respiratory failure on October 30, 1986, at St. John's Hospital in Jackson, Wyoming.)